Tracing Your Family History

A Step-by-Step Guide to

Tracing Your Family History

Marijke Alderson

Viking O'Neil

Viking O'Neil
Penguin Books Australia Ltd
487 Maroondah Highway, PO Box 257
Ringwood, Victoria 3134, Australia
Penguin Books Ltd
Harmondsworth, Middlesex, England
Viking Penguin Inc.
40 West 23rd Street, New York, N.Y. 10010, U.S.A.
Penguin Books Canada Limited
2801 John Street, Markham, Ontario, Canada L3R 1B4
Penguin Books (N.Z.) Ltd
182–190 Wairau Road, Auckland 10, New Zealand

First published by Penguin Books Australia Ltd 1988
10 9 8 7 6 5 4 3 2
Copyright © City of Caulfield, 1988

Produced by Viking O'Neil
56 Claremont Street, South Yarra, Victoria 3141, Australia
A division of Penguin Books Australia Ltd

Designed by William Hung
Illustrated by Lorraine Ellis
Typeset in Bembo and Optima by Bookset Pty Ltd, Victoria
Printed and bound by Globe Press Pty Ltd, Melbourne

National Library of Australia
Cataloguing-in-Publication data

Alderson, Marijke, 1947–
   A step-by-step guide to tracing your family history.

Bibliography.
ISBN 0 670 90112 1.

1. Australia – Genealogy. I. Title. II. Title:
Tracing your family history.

929'.1'0994

Foreword

With the availability in libraries of microfiche records from the various registries of births, deaths and marriages, many newcomers to genealogy and family history have begun to research their ancestry. All too often, however, they have been overwhelmed by the sheer volume of publications on the subject.

At the Caulfield Library Service, we became increasingly aware that many amateur family historians needed concrete assistance and guidance in the early stages of their research. This need led to Marijke Alderson's book, which assists beginners in the planning and organisation of their research and the documentation of the results. The book does not attempt to cover the same ground as the more specialised guides to genealogy; rather its aim is to provide a set of specially designed work forms and step-by-step guidance in their use.

The forms will help beginners to think about the goals they wish to achieve in researching their family history. They can choose to develop a pedigree chart for one line of their family, complete essential data on one couple and their children, or study an ancestor at some depth. Beginning the time-consuming but fascinating task of family research in an orderly manner will help amateur researchers to establish a good framework on which to build further. With more work they will be able to produce an absorbing family history, depicting the social mores of the period.

I wish readers happy and productive searching.

Gladys E. Vallati
Reference and Information Librarian, Caulfield Library Service

Contents

Forms

Figures

Tables

Acknowledgements

I wish to thank several people for their encouragement and assistance. Gladys Vallati, Reference and Information Librarian of the Caulfield Library Service, originally saw the need for the book, and her constant support, help, constructive criticism, editing and proofreading are greatly appreciated. Jim Badger, Co-ordinator of the Caulfield Library Service, arranged the financing of the book and, with Gladys Vallati, encouraged me in the writing of it.

Joan Wills, Honorary Research Officer of the Genealogical Society of Victoria, offered many helpful comments and criticisms, based on a wealth of genealogical knowledge. Jim Flahavin, Assistant Research Officer of the Genealogical Society of Victoria, also made many useful suggestions regarding the organisation of charts; his own chart forms the basis of the family data sheet provided in the book.

Donna Apaps, Training Librarian with the Church of Jesus Christ of Latter-day Saints, offered helpful comments and suggestions for items to be included in *Tracing Your Family History*.

Frances Brown, Genealogy and Local History Librarian with the La Trobe Collection of the State Library of Victoria and an author of genealogical books, offered constructive criticisms, based on her own writing experience, of the early draft of the book.

Mike and Yvonne Saunders, professional genealogical researchers, provided helpful information and gave me permission to use Mike's name index in my section on writing family histories.

Carol Harry, Community Liaison Officer with the Caulfield City Council, suggested that I send the book to outside publishers, rather than just produce an in-house publication.

Finally, my thanks go to Richard Alderson, my parents Bert and Hetta Van Driel, and my children Tineke and Janneke for their encouragement and their patience with me during the writing of this book.

Glossary

Archives: place where public or other records are stored.

Genealogy: study of ancestral descent and pedigree.

IGI: abbreviation for the *International Genealogical Index* – a microfiche collection of names compiled by the Church of Jesus Christ of Latter-day Saints. It covers every country in the world, mainly for the period before 1870. It contains only birth, baptism and marriage entries, not deaths, and includes those born at sea.

Microfiche: microfilmed transparency about the size and shape of a filing card, which may have on it many pages of print.

Microfilm: roll of film, usually 16 or 35 millimetres in length, on which documents have been recorded.

Pedigree chart: diagram showing a family's line of descent.

St Catherine's House Index: index to the holdings of St Catherine's House, London, which is the general registry office for births, deaths and marriages.

Introduction

Have you recently:

- wondered whether there was any truth in the family folklore that your ancestors were related to Ned Kelly?

- seen a copy of your great-grandfather's will and become curious about the people mentioned in it?

- discovered an intriguing photograph of Great-great-aunt Mary on a camel somewhere in the outback and now want to know the story behind it?

- felt that you would like to know what life was like for your pioneering ancestors in the Riverina?

If so, you are one of a growing number of Australians becoming increasingly interested in researching their family history.

Most of our families abound with rumours of famous or infamous ancestors, such as 'Clancy of the Overflow' or an unjustly sentenced convict, and the curiosity aroused by such stories is often enough to set us in pursuit of our forebears. As well, because we now live in small families in large cities, many of us feel the need to get in touch with our past, to discover our roots. Once we have 'caught the bug' of genealogical research we often find that it becomes a lifelong and fulfilling interest.

Tracing your family's origins is essentially fascinating detective work. It will have you:

- ransacking your attic for the family Bible

- browsing in libraries to discover whether the abbreviation 'Chil.' means your ancestor lived in Chilwell or Chiltern

- arranging assignations with a long-lost great-aunt to look at old photographs

- sending off to your State registry for your great-great-grandfather's marriage certificate.

But how to begin this fascinating detective work? At this point, despite your enthusiasm, you are probably confused about where to start and daunted by the task ahead. You probably suspect – quite rightly – that genealogical research takes time and effort and entails adhering to set procedures.

It's true that family history involves long hours consulting certain reference works in libraries, acquiring certain original documents and following certain practices of recording and organising information. However, the work can be very pleasurable and productive, and a great deal of frustration and wasted time can be avoided, if you know exactly what you should do at each stage. *Tracing Your Family History* has been written to give you the confidence that you can undertake family research yourself and to help you commence and continue such work. Its aims are to:

- answer all your questions about how to undertake family research

- provide you with a system for organising findings

- offer you a clear guide to the logical steps that you need to follow to complete your research successfully.

Tracing Your Family History is a book for beginners who are interested in following their family's fortunes in Australia. Although it suggests the lines you will need to follow if you are interested in tracing your family in its country of origin, it is not primarily concerned with the use of such overseas genealogical sources as parish registers and the *International Genealogical Index*. If, when you have completed the steps outlined in the book, you want to explore further into the past, you will find that you have sufficient expertise and knowledge to undertake confidently the more specialised research required.

Tracing Your Family History assumes that you will probably be interested in:

- outlining your family's pedigree, that is, recording the names and life event dates of all the members of one line of your family, on a generational basis, and/or

- following up one particular ancestor, and/or

- writing, and perhaps publishing, your family history.

It therefore discusses each of these aspects of genealogy in turn and gives you a step-by-step guide to achieving your aim. Part I tells you how to:

- use family, library and genealogical society resources

- obtain crucial documents

- record and organise your information

- write, and perhaps publish, your family history.

    To help you organise your findings Part I provides:

- a complete set of data forms to photocopy, which includes a pedigree chart and a research log

- sample letters requesting information

- copies of the official documents with which you need to become familiar.

In Part II you will find the addresses and other details of all the organisations discussed in Part I. At the end of the book Further Reading lists and discusses works that will be of use to you if you wish to read further or go into more depth at a particular stage in your research; publishing details for the main works mentioned in *Tracing Your Family History* are also given here.

To demonstrate, in a lively and concrete way, how a family history is gradually fleshed out the book uses the example of a fictitious family – the Sagars – throughout.

The basic steps

There are six fundamental questions that you need to ask as you undertake your research. Throughout *Tracing Your Family History* these questions are raised at each step to help you approach your task in an orderly and logical manner.

1 *What do I want to learn about my family?*
2 *What do I already know about my family and how do I record it?*
3 *What information do I have at home?*
4 *What records do libraries, genealogical societies and other organisations have?*
5 *How do I obtain the records I want?*
6 *Where do I go from here?*

1 What do I want to learn about my family?
Before commencing your research, you need to have a clear idea of what you would like to discover. Until you have defined your aim you will not be able to plan your approach. As already suggested, you may wish to record your family's pedigree, follow up one ancestor or write a detailed family history.

2 What do I know already about my family and how do I record it?
You need to remember that you already know a lot about your family before you even begin work. As Chapter 1 discusses, it is important to record this information first: you will then be able to see what further research is required.

3 What information do I have at home?
Some of your best sources of genealogical information may be records you already have at home: the family Bible, old letters, diaries, school records, wills and personal certificates, such as birth, death and marriage certificates. You may need to write to or visit relatives to locate some family possessions.

4 What records do libraries, genealogical societies and other organisations have?
Records at your local or State library, government archives and departments and genealogical societies will provide you with further information. As Chapter 3 discusses at greater length, the records basically fall into two categories:

- results of previous research into families

- original documents or information about them.

5 How do I obtain the records I want?
Personal documents, such as birth, death and marriage certificates, are the most important documents you will need in researching your family. Details are given in Chapter 3 about where to obtain them and in Chapter 4 about how to acquire them.

6 Where do I go from here?
Finally, you need to evaluate the information you already have to establish what additional information you would like to have and what sources need to be followed up. Tackle any further research as you approached your initial enquiries, that is, by working through the six basic questions.

Note: it is easiest to start with what you know and already have, therefore it is preferable to work through the six questions in sequence. However, questions 3 and 4 may be interchanged if you are in a library, and not at home, when you begin your research.

Since you will probably find it easiest to commence your work by recording your family's pedigree and essential details about your immediate family, *Tracing Your Family History* begins with a discussion of how to go about this.

Part I

Organising and recording your family history

Join a genealogical society. You will find its talks, seminars, conferences and field days very enjoyable and instructive.

1

Using pedigree charts and family data sheets

What do I want to learn about my family?
As suggested in the Introduction, a good starting point for your research is the recording of your family's pedigree and all the details about your immediate family.

What do I already know about my family and how do I record it?
You will probably already know a lot about your family. It is important to note down what you do know before you progress further. This enables you to see what information requires verification and what gaps there are.

The best way to start is by filling in as much detail as you can on genealogical charts. Using a chart will ensure that you organise your findings about your family's pedigree in an orderly fashion. A variety of genealogical charts exist.

Genealogical charts

Drop or vertical chart

This chart (see Figure 1) shows all the descendants of a couple. (Note that in *Tracing Your Family History* the family data sheet discussed later in the chapter provides similar information, although not in chart form.) The advantages of the drop chart are that:

- it shows brothers and sisters (which the pedigree chart, discussed below, does not)

- it is very useful when you are writing about a particular person or particular generation (see Chapters 5 and 6).

The disadvantages are that:

- it can be easily overloaded if, for example, four brothers marry and each has seven children, all of whom marry, and so on

- unless great care is taken to keep the entries for each member of the one generation aligned on the chart, it is easy to confuse the generations.

Figure 1: Drop or vertical chart

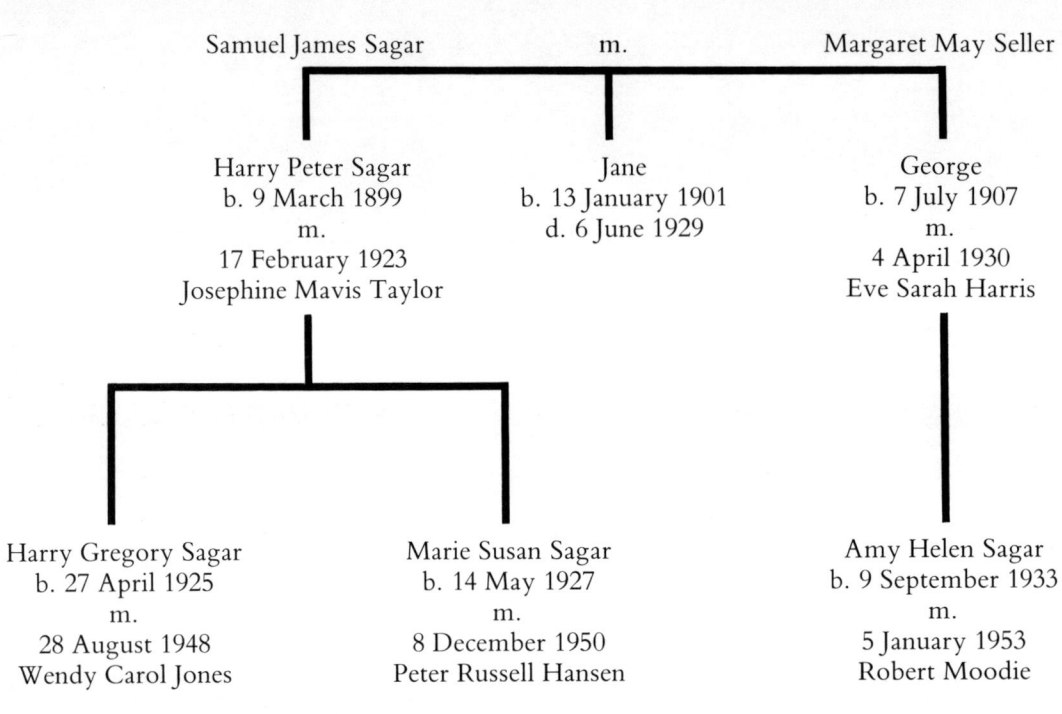

Narrative chart

This is a more descriptive form of chart than the others (see Figure 2). Its advantages are that:

- it is a useful alternative to diagrammatic charts when you are writing a family history

- you can include more personal details about family members.

Its disadvantage is that:

- it can be very hard to follow when a large family is involved.

SAMUEL JAMES SAGAR, b. Chiltern, Victoria, 27 September 1876; m. Chiltern, 1 March 1896, Margaret May, daughter of James Seller; d. Chiltern, 5 June 1930, leaving issue:

1 HARRY PETER, b. Chiltern, Victoria, 9 March 1899; became a blacksmith at Williamstown, Victoria; m. Chiltern, 17 February 1923, Josephine Mavis, daughter of Henry Taylor; d. Chiltern, 4 May 1945, leaving issue:

   1 Harry Gregory, b. Williamstown, Victoria, 27 April 1925; m. Williamstown, 28 August 1948, Wendy Carol Jones.
   2 Marie Susan, b. Williamstown, Victoria, 14 May 1927; m. Williamstown, 8 December 1950, Peter Russell Hansen.

2 JANE, b. Chiltern, Victoria, 13 January 1901; became a seamstress in Chiltern; d. unmarried Chiltern, 6 June 1929.

3 GEORGE, b. Chiltern, Victoria, 7 July 1907; m. Chiltern, 4 April 1930, Eve Sarah Harris; issue:

   Amy Helen, b. Chiltern, Victoria, 9 September 1933; m. Williamstown, 5 January 1953, Robert Moodie.

Wheel chart

This chart is circular in form (see Figure 3). You start in the centre, with either a member of the most recent generation or one from the oldest, and draw family lines out from there. (In Figure 3 the chart starts with Adam Peter Sagar, a member of the most recent generation of our fictitious Sagar family.) The advantages of the chart are that:

- it looks superb, for example, as a wall hanging when drawn well

- it can become a central feature of a family history, although other, more detailed, charts may need to be included also.

Its disadvantages are that:

- it is not very useful for recording general information, such as birth, marriage and death dates and places

- it does not provide for any side branches, such as the families of the brothers and sisters of the central member.

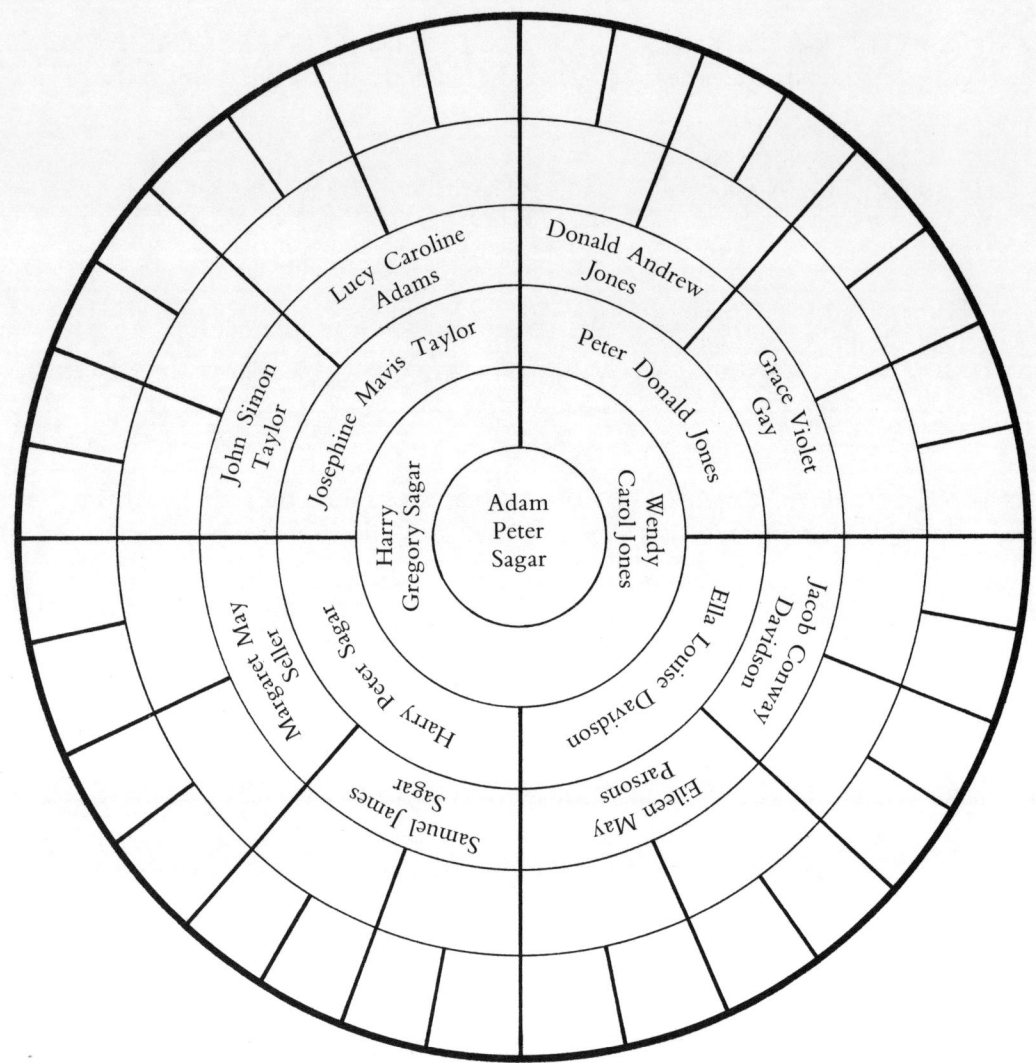

Family tree

This chart consists of a drawing of a tree upon whose branches the names and details of family members are recorded (see Figure 4). It may be accompanied by photographs. Its advantages are that:

- it is a striking illustration which, like the wheel chart, looks good on a wall

- it is useful for family reunions.

    Its disadvantages are that:

- if it is to be done well, it requires artistic talent

- because of its size it is not suitable for inclusion in a family history.

Figure 4: Family tree

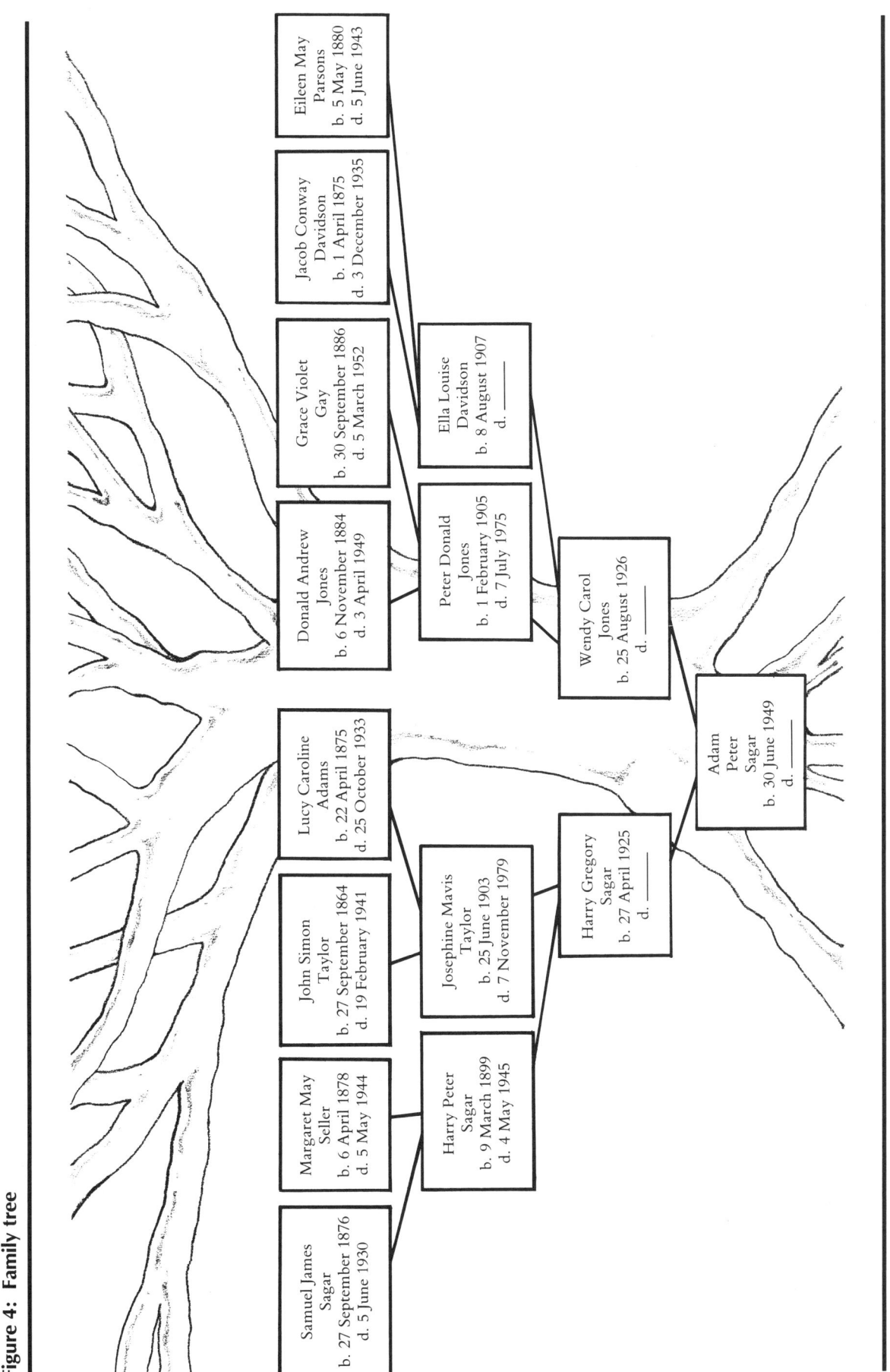

Eileen May
Parsons
b. 5 May 1880
d. 5 June 1943

Jacob Conway
Davidson
b. 1 April 1875
d. 3 December 1935

Grace Violet
Gay
b. 30 September 1886
d. 5 March 1952

Ella Louise
Davidson
b. 8 August 1907
d. _____

Donald Andrew
Jones
b. 6 November 1884
d. 3 April 1949

Peter Donald
Jones
b. 1 February 1905
d. 7 July 1975

Wendy Carol
Jones
b. 25 August 1926
d. _____

Lucy Caroline
Adams
b. 22 April 1875
d. 25 October 1933

John Simon
Taylor
b. 27 September 1864
d. 19 February 1941

Josephine Mavis
Taylor
b. 25 June 1903
d. 7 November 1979

Harry Gregory
Sagar
b. 27 April 1925
d. _____

Adam
Peter
Sagar
b. 30 June 1949
d. _____

Samuel James
Sagar
b. 27 September 1876
d. 5 June 1930

Margaret May
Seller
b. 6 April 1878
d. 5 May 1944

Harry Peter
Sagar
b. 9 March 1899
d. 4 May 1945

Portrait pedigree chart

This looks like the horizontal chart discussed below, but the information boxes are used for photographs. Its advantages are that:

- it makes a horizontal chart more interesting when the two are used together

- it is a valuable addition to a family history.

    Its disadvantage is that:

- it does not leave much room for recording details, such as dates.

A portrait pedigree chart (Form A) is included in this chapter for you to photocopy and use. (You may wish to enlarge it on the photocopying machine.) Remember to write the name of each family member below his or her photograph.

Pedigree or horizontal chart

This type of chart reads from left to right, starting with a member of the most recent generation. It shows only the direct line of ancestry (see Form B). For our purposes the pedigree chart is the most useful because:

- it is simple to read – you can see each generation at a glance

- details, such as birth, death and marriage dates and places, are easily recorded on it

- it is easy to include in any letter you write to family members or a genealogical society requesting further information

- it provides a clear and detailed index to known information

- it provides a guide for further research because you can see at a glance what information gaps exist.

How to use the pedigree chart

The pedigree chart included in this chapter (see Form B):

- starts with you in the left-hand column and works through your parents and grandparents to your eight great-grandparents on the right

Form A: Portrait pedigree chart of the descendants of _____

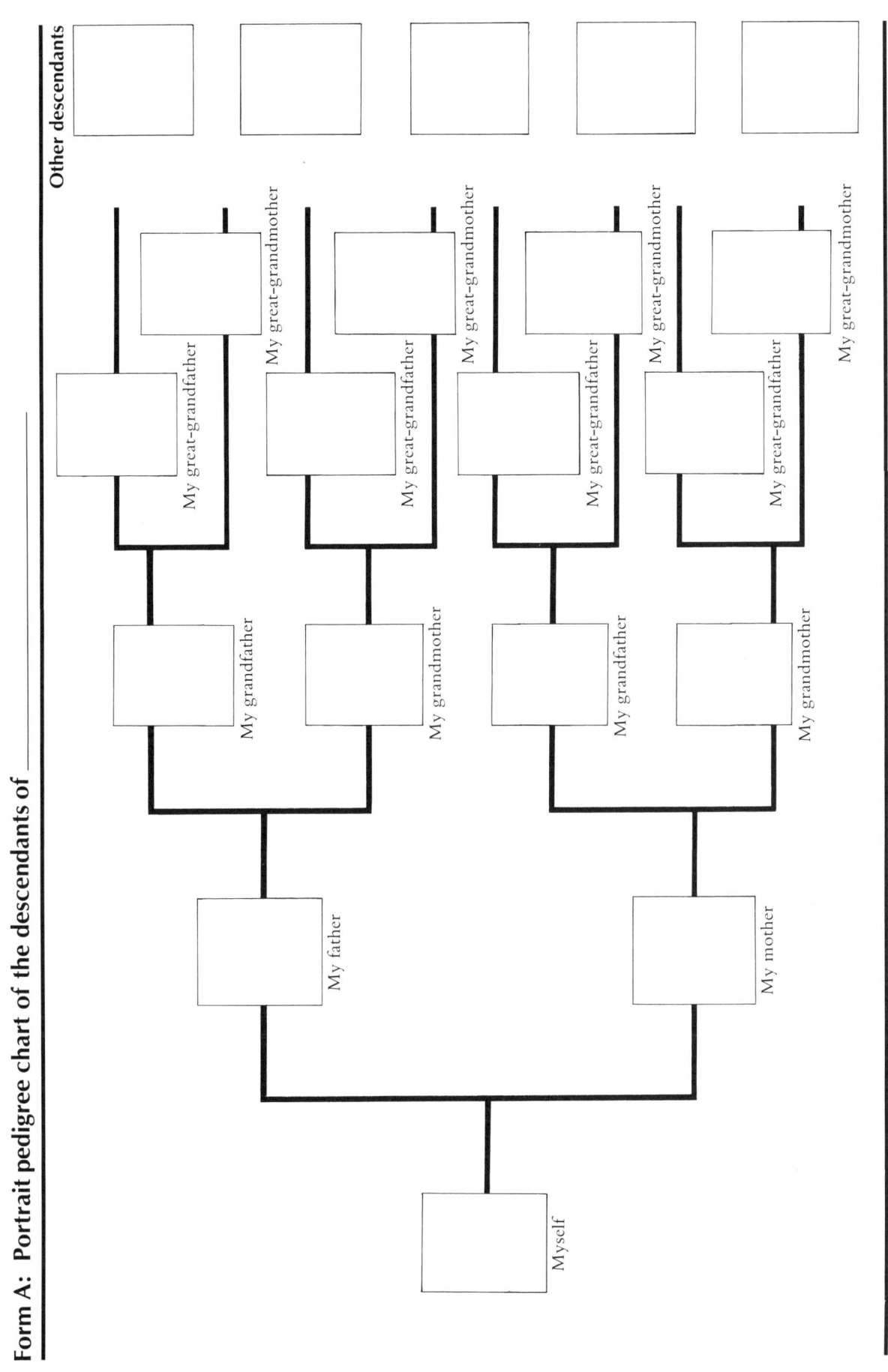

Other descendants

My great-grandmother

My great-grandfather

My great-grandmother

My great-grandfather

My great-grandmother

My great-grandfather

My great-grandmother

My great-grandfather

My grandfather

My grandmother

My grandfather

My grandmother

My father

My mother

Myself

- provides spaces for you to record the name and the birth, marriage and death dates and places for each member of the last four generations (note that a four-generation chart, rather than the usual five-generation one, has been chosen to allow more space for information, such as place of marriage)

- gives each family member a number (to make it easier for you to refer to him or her in the 'Sources of information' space and elsewhere): you are number 1 and the even numbers from 2 to 14 refer to the males in your family, while the odd numbers from 3 to 15 refer to the females

- provides a space in the left-hand column for 'Sources of information', that is, for you to record briefly where you obtained your details about particular family members (how to number items correctly is explained in 'Filling in the home sources form', Chapter 2)

- gives places in the right-hand column for you to refer to any additional pedigree charts used, if you have followed your pedigree back beyond the four generations (see the discussion later in this chapter on organising further pedigree charts).

Note that in the column for your great-grandparents provision has been made for you to enter baptism and burial dates in cases where births and deaths occurred before official records were kept. Church records may be all that are available.

Filling in your pedigree chart

[1] Photocopy Form B for your use.

[2] Fill in as much information as you can from memory – of course there will be many blank spaces initially, but as you further your research (see the discussion in Chapters 2–4) you will be able to add steadily to your pedigree chart.

[3] Keep recorded information simple. Record only details such as dates and places. Other information, for example details of occupation, will overload the chart, and provision for it has been made on the family data sheet (see the following discussion).

[4] Print clearly in black ink.

[5] Record names in full, that is, both family and given names.

[6] Record maiden names for married women.

[7] Write dates in full to avoid confusion (for example, 3 July 1987).

Form B: Pedigree chart

Chart 1

1 (Myself) _____

Born _____

Where _____

Married _____

Where _____

Name of husband or wife

_____

Sources of information
(Give name of record where
information obtained. Refer to family
members by number.)

2 _____

Born _____

Where _____

Married _____

Where _____

Died _____

Where _____

3 _____

Born _____

Where _____

Died _____

Where _____

4 _____

Born _____

Where _____

Married _____

Where _____

Died _____

Where _____

5 _____

Born _____

Where _____

Died _____

Where _____

6 _____

Born _____

Where _____

Married _____

Where _____

Died _____

Where _____

7 _____

Born _____

Where _____

Died _____

Where _____

8 _____

Born/baptised _____

Married _____

Died/buried _____

Continued on chart _____

Where _____

Where _____

Where _____

9 _____

Born/baptised _____

Died/buried _____

Continued on chart _____

Where _____

Where _____

10 _____

Born/baptised _____

Married _____

Died/buried _____

Continued on chart _____

Where _____

Where _____

Where _____

11 _____

Born/baptised _____

Died/buried _____

Continued on chart _____

Where _____

Where _____

12 _____

Born/baptised _____

Married _____

Died/buried _____

Continued on chart _____

Where _____

Where _____

Where _____

13 _____

Born/baptised _____

Died/buried _____

Continued on chart _____

Where _____

Where _____

14 _____

Born/baptised _____

Married _____

Died/buried _____

Continued on chart _____

Where _____

Where _____

Where _____

15 _____

Born/baptised _____

Died/buried _____

Continued on chart _____

Where _____

Where _____

8 Write in: city, town or suburb; State; and country, if not Australia.

9 If you are uncertain of a date put down a rough estimate and verify it later.

10 As a guide, use the filled-in sample of a pedigree chart provided (see Figure 5), which follows the last four generations of the Sagars. (The sample contains more information than you would be able to supply from memory, of course, to give you an idea of how a pedigree chart is built up.)

Special problems

- Adopted children: trace the tree of the adopted family unless the natural parents are known to the family.

- Illegitimate children: usually these children use the mother's maiden name; the natural father may not be recorded or known.

- Multi-marriages: these are listed on the family data sheet (see the following discussion) because the pedigree chart does not record prior or subsequent marriages. One family data sheet is used for each marriage.

Family data sheet

The family data sheet (see Form C) is used for the immediate family of yourself or an ancestor, with children and all their details recorded. One family data sheet is used for each couple. It is very useful because, as an extension of one section of your pedigree chart, it acts as a starting point for further research and provides an index of known information.

Filling in your family data sheet

1 Photocopy Form C for your use.

2 Fill in the surname of the family you are researching after 'Research line' on the top left-hand side.

3 In the spaces provided for 'Husband's genealogy number' and 'Wife's genealogy number', at the top of the form, enter the numbers assigned to both partners on your pedigree chart (Form B).

4 Give your own name in the 'Compiled by' space and record the date on which you fill out the form.

Figure 5: Sample pedigree chart (Form B)

Chart 1

8 Samuel James Sagar
Born/baptised 1870s
Married 1 March 1896
Died/buried 5 June 1930
Continued on chart ___2___
Where ___
Where ___
Where ___

9 Margaret May Seller
Born/baptised 6 April 1878
Died/buried 5 May 1944
Continued on chart ___
Where ___
Where ___

10 John Simon Taylor
Born/baptised 27 Sept. 1864
Married 5 July 1895
Died/buried 19 Feb. 1941
Continued on chart ___
Where ___
Where ___
Where ___

11 Lucy Caroline Adams
Born/baptised 22 April 1875
Died/buried 25 October 1933
Continued on chart ___
Where ___
Where ___

12 Donald Andrew Jones
Born/baptised 6 Nov. 1884
Married 1 January 1904
Died/buried 3 April 1949
Continued on chart ___
Where ___
Where ___
Where ___

13 Grace Violet Gay
Born/baptised 30 Sept. 1886
Died/buried 5 March 1952
Continued on chart ___
Where ___
Where ___

14 Jacob Conway Davidson
Born/baptised 1 April 1875
Married 13 April 1905
Died/buried 3 Dec. 1935
Continued on chart ___
Where ___
Where ___
Where ___

15 Eileen May Parsons
Born/baptised 5 May 1880
Died/buried 5 June 1943
Continued on chart ___
Where ___
Where ___

4 Harry Peter Sagar
Born 9 March 1899
Where Chiltern, Vic.
Married 17 February 1923
Where Chiltern
Died 4 May 1945
Where Chiltern

5 Josephine Mavis Taylor
Born 25 June 1903
Where Chiltern
Died 7 November 1979
Where Chiltern

6 Peter Donald Jones
Born 1 February 1905
Where ___
Married 7 February 1925
Where ___
Died 7 July 1975
Where ___

7 Ella Louise Davidson
Born 8 August 1907
Where ___
Died ___
Where ___

2 Harry Gregory Sagar
Born 27 April 1925
Where Williamstown, Vic.
Married 28 August 1948
Where Williamstown, Vic.
Died ___
Where ___

3 Wendy Carol Jones
Born 25 August 1926
Where Williamstown, Vic.
Died ___
Where ___

1 (Myself) Adam Peter Sagar
Born 30 June 1949
Where Ballarat, Victoria
Married 16 October 1972
Where Melbourne, Victoria
Name of husband or wife
Suzanne Mary Taylor

Sources of information
(Give name of record where
information obtained. Refer to family
members by number.)

4 Birth certificate (item 3-1)

5 Birth certificate (item 3-2)

2,3 Marriage certificate (item 4-1)

Form C: Family data sheet

Research line _____

Compiled by _____

Date _____

Husband's genealogy number _____

Wife's genealogy number _____

Husband's name _____

Wife's maiden name _____

Birth _____ Place _____

Baptism _____ Place _____

Marriage _____ Place _____

Birth _____ Place _____

Baptism _____ Place _____

Marriage _____ Place _____

Other wives _____

Other husbands _____

Death _____ Place _____

Burial _____ Place _____

Death _____ Place _____

Burial _____ Place _____

Father's name _____

Mother's maiden name _____

Occupation _____

Address _____

Telephone number _____

Father's name _____

Mother's maiden name _____

Occupation _____

Address _____

Telephone number _____

Sheet _____

Seq. no.	Children's names	When and where born	When and where married	Married to	Issue	When and where died

Sources of information

5 Give the husband's and wife's full names, work ('Occupation'), present or final address and the names of any other spouses – additional marriages must then be recorded on separate family data sheets.

6 Name all the children of the marriage in order of birth, recording their 'Seq. no.' (sequential number), and fill in their details – 'Issue' refers to the number of offspring each child has.

7 Record your 'Sources of information', as you did for your pedigree chart.

8 As a guide, use the filled-in sample of a family data sheet (see Figure 6), which uses the example of the immediate family of Adam Sagar's father and mother.

9 File your family data sheet with its relevant pedigree chart and any other information you may have about the particular family, such as certificates and photographs.

Organising further pedigree charts

If you wish to trace your ancestors back beyond your great-grandparents you will require more than your initial pedigree chart (Form B) and perhaps several family data sheets (Form Cs).

Filling in additional pedigree charts

1 To your first pedigree chart add eight blank, four-generation pedigree charts by photocopying Form D, which is the same as Form B except that the left-hand space is reserved, not for you, but for one of the great-grandparents recorded on your first chart.

2 Number the additional eight charts from 2 to 9 at the top right-hand corner (number 1 is, of course, your initial pedigree chart).

3 On the right-hand side of pedigree chart 1 you will find eight lines labelled 'Continued on chart —'. Give each space a number from 2 to 9, numbering from the top to the bottom. These numbers will refer you to the pedigree chart on which the details of a particular great-grandparent are continued.

4 Commence filling out pedigree chart 2, which is the chart allotted to great-grandparent number 8 on pedigree chart 1. (In Figure 5 this is Samuel James Sagar, so his name is given in the left-hand column of pedigree chart 2 and it is recorded that 'The first person on this chart is number 8 on pedigree chart 1'.)

Figure 6: Sample family data sheet (Form C)

Research line _Sagar Family_

Compiled by _Adam Sagar_

Date _3 May 1987_

Husband's genealogy number _2_

Wife's genealogy number _3_

Husband's name _Harry Gregory Sagar_

Wife's maiden name _Wendy Carol Jones_

Birth _27 April 1925_ Place _Williamstown, Victoria_

Birth _25 August 1926_ Place _Williamstown, Victoria_

Baptism _____ Place _____

Baptism _____ Place _____

Marriage _28 August 1948_ Place _Williamstown, Victoria_

Marriage _28 August 1948_ Place _Williamstown, Victoria_

Other wives _Nil_

Other husbands _Nil_

Death _____ Place _____

Death _____ Place _____

Burial _____ Place _____

Burial _____ Place _____

Father's name _Harry Peter Sagar_

Father's name _Peter Donald Jones_

Mother's maiden name _Josephine Mavis Taylor_

Mother's maiden name _Ella Louise Davidson_

Occupation _Teacher_

Occupation _Home duties_

Address _Smith Street, Ballarat, Victoria_

Address _Smith Street, Ballarat, Victoria_

Telephone number _____

Telephone number _____

Seq. no.	Children's names	When and where born	When and where married	Married to	Issue	When and where died
1	Adam Peter Sagar	30 June 1949, Ballarat, Vic.	16 Oct. 1972, Melbourne, Vic.	Suzanne Mary Taylor	3	
2	Phillip Roy Sagar	5 May 1951, Ballarat, Vic.	3 Sept. 1980, Melbourne, Vic.	Wendy Louise Dixon	1	

Sources of information

Marriage certificate (item 4-1, home sources form)

Family Bible (item 1, home sources form)

Diary (item 5-1, home sources form)

Photograph album (item 6-1, home sources form)

5 Complete pedigree chart 2 as you did 1, giving each ancestor a number – these numbers will begin at 16, where the numbers of the family members recorded on pedigree chart 1 ended.

6 Fill out the remaining pedigree charts (3 to 9) in the same way that you have pedigree chart 2.

Of course you will not be able to fill in every detail on each sheet until you have undertaken the research discussed in Chapters 2–4.

Note: further organisation of charts is a subject on its own. If you wish to trace your family back beyond seven generations you will usually find it necessary to undertake research in Great Britain or other countries. This work is beyond the scope of *Tracing Your Family History*, so you will need to do additional reading. You should also join a genealogical society (see Chapters 3 and 10). Attend its seminars and talks on organisation of material and discuss various methods with very experienced genealogists.

Form D: Pedigree chart continued

Chart _____

The first person on this chart is number ____ on pedigree chart ____

Born _____
Where _____
Married _____
Where _____
Name of husband or wife _____
_____

Sources of information
(Give name of record where information obtained. Refer to family members by number.)

Born _____
Where _____
Married _____
Where _____
Died _____
Where _____

Born _____
Where _____
Died _____
Where _____

Born _____
Where _____
Married _____
Where _____
Died _____
Where _____

Born _____
Where _____
Died _____
Where _____

Born/baptised _____
Married _____
Died/buried _____

Continued on chart _____
Where _____
Where _____
Where _____

Born/baptised _____
Died/buried _____

Continued on chart _____
Where _____
Where _____

Born/baptised _____
Married _____
Died/buried _____

Continued on chart _____
Where _____
Where _____
Where _____

Born/baptised _____
Died/buried _____

Continued on chart _____
Where _____
Where _____

Born/baptised _____
Married _____
Died/buried _____

Continued on chart _____
Where _____
Where _____
Where _____

Born/baptised _____
Died/buried _____

Continued on chart _____
Where _____
Where _____

Born/baptised _____
Married _____
Died/buried _____

Continued on chart _____
Where _____
Where _____
Where _____

Born/baptised _____
Died/buried _____

Continued on chart _____
Where _____
Where _____

2

Using home and family sources

Having filled in a pedigree chart (Form B) and family data sheet (Form C) with what you already know, it is time to seek further for information. The best place to start is at home. There are many home sources from which genealogical information may be gleaned and many items that will help you fill in the gaps on the charts you have already commenced. Contacting family members can be very rewarding, also. The second half of the chapter is therefore concerned with how to write to relatives, how to interview them and how to organise family reunions.

What information do I have at home?
The best starting point is original documents, such as birth, death and marriage certificates. Original documents are those recorded at the time of the event. Therefore they are generally your most accurate sources of information. Look for copies of the following:

- your birth certificate

- your parents' marriage certificate

- your parents' birth certificates

- your grandparents' marriage certificate

- your grandparents' birth certificates

- your great-grandparents' marriage certificate

- your great-grandparents' birth certificates.

However, although these certificates are highly important, there are many other useful family documents and possessions, as Table 1 demonstrates.

Table 1: Home sources

Memorabilia	family Bible, letters, birthday books, baby books, wedding books, diaries, visitors books, yearbooks, scrapbooks, newspaper clippings, obituaries, cemetery information, medals, trophies, paintings
Legal documents	deeds, titles, land grants, mortgages, leases, contracts, business papers, wills, naturalisation papers
Personal documents	union papers, passports, divorce papers, medical records, service records
Personal certificates	birth, marriage, death and baptism certificates
Educational documents	graduation certificates or papers, apprenticeship certificates, school reports, school magazines
Financial documents	taxation, bank and insurance papers
Books	biographies, family histories, local histories
Photographs	framed photographs, albums of photographs

Organisation of home sources

The sources you find need to be sorted and organised so that you obtain maximum benefit from their contents. The home sources form provided in this chapter (see Form E) will help you record them systematically. It:

- records home and family sources and their location

- allocates a number to all items so that they may be referred to briefly on other forms such as the pedigree chart (Form B) and the family data sheet (Form C)

- provides a summary of the sources you and your family have, to eliminate the need to sort through them repeatedly

- gives the location of documents at a glance.

Filling in the home sources form

[1] Photocopy Form E for your use.

[2] As a guide, refer to the filled-in sample of a home sources form (Figure 7).

3 Record each item in the column provided.

4 If appropriate, write a brief description of each item: for example, give the names of writer and recipient for letters.

5 Record the location of each item – if your Aunt Mary owns the family Bible, you will need to give her address and telephone number.

6 Give each item a number so that you can refer to it easily on other forms, such as the pedigree chart and the family data sheet. You will see that in Figure 7 each letter has been allotted the prefix 2. The number that follows refers to the particular writer. Thus the letter of Samuel James Sagar to Margaret May Seller is 2–1 and that of Margaret May Seller to Samuel James Sagar is 2–2. Further letters written by Samuel James Sagar would be numbered 2–1a, 2–1b and so on.

Figure 7: Sample home sources form (Form E)

Item	Description	Location	Item no.
Family Bible		Mrs A. Sagar 2 Bay Street Rowville VICTORIA	1
Letters	Samuel James Sagar to Margaret May Seller	Desk	2-1
	Margaret Seller to Samuel Sagar	"	2-2
	Harry Peter Sagar to Margaret Seller	"	2-3
Birth certificates	Harry Peter Sagar	Filing Cabinet	3-1
	Josephine Mavis Taylor	"	3-2
Marriage certificate	Harry Gregory Sagar and Wendy Carol Jones	Filing Cabinet	4-1
Diary	Harry Gregory Sagar	Trunk in spare room	5-1
Photograph album	Harry Gregory Sagar	Bookcase	6-1

Preserving home sources

File home sources in folders where appropriate. Use plastic envelopes for photographs or fragile items, such as very old letters and cards. Plastic envelopes must be of the acid-free type.

Important photographs may be further preserved by arranging to have them photographed or touched up (this will cost more). Where possible you should record names, date and place in pencil on the back of the photograph.

Form E: Home sources

Item	Description	Location	Item no.

Using home sources information

- Record the information that you have obtained about names, dates and places on your pedigree chart and family data sheet.

- Record the number of any item used to provide information for the pedigree chart and family data sheet in their 'Sources of information' spaces. For example, the filled-in sample of a home sources form (see Figure 7) records that the Sagar home possesses Harry Peter Sagar's birth certificate: when you turn back to the filled-in sample of a pedigree chart (see Figure 5) you will see that the certificate's information has been recorded in Harry Peter Sagar's space and that its number (3–1) has been entered under 'Sources of information'.

- Check what gaps are still left on your forms, that is, what information you still require. This done, it is time to contact family members.

Note: because at this stage your aim is to write your family pedigree and perhaps to record the basic data about your own or an ancestor's immediate family, you are seeking names, dates and places; however, home and family sources also contain other information, such as details of members' occupations and interests, which will be important if you plan to write the history of one member or of the family. Chapter 6 discusses how to organise and use family sources further.

Writing letters

Writing letters asking for information to family members is an important method of furthering your research. However, the amount and value of the information you receive will depend largely on how clearly you express your needs in your letter. It is important to remember that, as this may be your initial and perhaps only contact with the receiver of your letter, the first impression is paramount. Therefore the following rules of good correspondence should be kept in mind.

1. Write clearly and concisely. Ask for only one or two items of information at a time and keep the letter brief. A clear request is much more likely to be met promptly than one which is buried in a maze of other, often irrelevant, writing.
   Never ask someone for everything they have.

2. Be reasonable and courteous. You are requesting information which you will only receive with the recipient's co-operation so do not be demanding. Express your appreciation for the trouble the person will take. The best way to ensure that your letter sounds reasonable and courteous is to put yourself in the place of the recipient.

You will often find valuable information contained in family possessions, such as certificates, wills, photograph albums and the family Bible.

3 Put in whatever relevant information you already have. An attached copy of your pedigree chart is ideal. In this way information will not be duplicated by the person to whom you are writing. As well, it will give the recipient the opportunity to verify your findings.

It is also most important to offer to share whatever other information you have, as an act of good faith and friendship.

4 Type the letter if possible. Otherwise, write legibly in black or blue ink. Again this will create a good impression and will facilitate the recipient's co-operation far more than an untidy, sloppy, illegible letter would do.

5 Always meet the cost of a reply yourself. This is a small but important courtesy that will facilitate the exchange of information.

If writing to someone in the same country, enclose a large, stamped, self-addressed envelope. If you are requesting information from someone overseas, you will need to include in your letter either postage stamps for the country of destination, purchased from stamp dealers or genealogical societies, or an international money order.

International money orders (see Figure 8) are exchangeable for postage stamps in any country of the Universal Postal Union and are available from your local post office. One coupon is required for an unregistered letter sent by surface mail. Two coupons are required for an airmail letter. More coupons may be required if anything additional is to be included in the return letter, for example, photocopies. International money orders may only be redeemed in the form of stamps, never in money, and are valid for approximately one year.

6 Keep copies of your correspondence and file them. Use lever-arch folders or manila folders, suitably divided, and keep all related inward and outward correspondence together. Extract all relevant information from the letters you receive and immediately record it on your charts. Remember to number the replies and to record them on your home sources form.

Figure 8: International money order

UNION POSTALE UNIVERSELLE   **COUPON-REPONSE INTERNATIONAL**   C 22

Ce coupon est échangeable dans tous les pays de l'Union postale universelle contre un ou plusieurs timbres-poste représentant l'affranchissement minimal d'une lettre ordinaire, expédiée à l'étranger par voie de surface.

Empreinte de contrôle du pays d'origine	Prix de vente (indication facultative)	Timbre du bureau qui effectue l'échange

The sample letters included here (see Figures 9 and 10) may be used as a guide for your letter writing. Figure 9 is a request for specific information about one ancestor; Figure 10 is a later letter asking for further, more detailed information.

Your letter writing will not always be restricted to contacting family members. Other people, such as friends and work associates of the ancestor you are interested in, may have additional information. To take your research further afield you can also place advertisements in newspapers. For example, the 'Help needed' column in the Melbourne *Age* (see Figure 11) achieves excellent results.

Figure 9: Letter requesting specific information about one ancestor

Name   Date
Address

Dear _____

I am attempting to trace the ancestry of the _____ family. At
present there are many gaps in the pedigree chart I have and I hope you may be able
to supply me with some of the missing information.

I am interested in _____ who was born
approximately _____ and I would like to know his/her details of
birth, marriage and death, that is, dates, locations, whom he/she married and so on.
As you are his/her nearest relative I would be most grateful if you could send me
these details, preferably in the form of copies of birth, marriage and death certificates
or whatever source of information you may have.

I have enclosed a stamped, addressed envelope for your reply. I would be happy to
reimburse you for any expenses, such as copying costs, that you may incur.

Thank you, in anticipation, for your help and co-operation.

Yours sincerely

Figure 10: Letter requesting more general information

Name   Date
Address

Dear _____
I am interested in tracing the pedigree and history of the _____
family. As my knowledge of your branch of the family is limited, I hope that you
will be able to provide me with the missing information.

I have enclosed a pedigree chart of the four most recent generations of my family so
that you can see the extent of my research. You may be interested in the family
details I have established. I have also enclosed a blank pedigree chart so that you can
fill in details about your branch of the family, as soon as it is convenient. Your
assistance will be greatly appreciated.

I have enclosed a stamped, addressed envelope for your reply. Should you know of
any others who could assist me, could you please send me their names and
addresses.

If you are interested in any of the families recorded on the filled-in pedigree chart
enclosed, I will be happy to send you further information about them.

Thank you, in anticipation, for your help and co-operation.

Yours sincerely

Figure 11: Melbourne *Age* 'Help needed' column

HELP NEEDED

A service for readers and researchers seeking specific information.

ULLAPOOL or Loch Broom: Information is sought about descendants of people who emigrated from Ullapool or Loch Broom, Western Ross, Scotland, for the Ullapool Bicentenary. Please contact Mrs R A McKenzie, 'Carnoch', 16 West Argyle Street, Ullapool, IV26 2TY, Ross-shire, Scotland.

ANDERSON: Information is sought about Henry John Anderson, born Kirkaldy, Scotland, 1806 and died 1878. He married Julia Lyall in Geelong in 1841. Their children were Alexander, John, Henry, Helen, James and Julia. Henry settled in Ballarat. Please contact Magaret Carty, RMB 7265, Hamilton, 3300. Telephone (055) 788201.

WINTHER: Information is sought about Winther cars. In 1921 or 1922, 500 Winther cars were imported to Australia from the US. None have survived in the US so any in Australia would have significant value. Please contact Grahame Ward, Box 383, Surfers Paradise, 4217.

HOWDENS, Smeatons, Silverwoods: Information is sought about any members of these families and their ancestors. Please contact Anne Holloway(Friends of Whitburgh Cottage), 3 George Street, Kilmore, 3764. Telephone (057) 821353.

KENNEDY: Information is sought about descendants of J Kennedy who married Emily Jean Park, and lived in Ferntree Gully around 1880-1920. Their children are thought to have been Olive, James and Thomas. Olive visited England in the 1940s. Please contact Mr G Lewis, 6 Milton Crescent, Tavistock, Devon, England, PL19 9AL.

PALESTINE: Information is sought about all members of the Australian Armed Forces who served in Palestine from 1922-1948. Please contact Fred O'Neill, 18 Redbourne Avenue, Mount Eliza, 3930. Telephone 7876775.

ROWBOTTOM: Information is sought about any descendants of the name Rowbottom which can be traced back to the Kings of Medieval Italy, via Germany, the North of England and London. Please contact Mr Frank Rowbottom, 37 Wrench Street, Cambridge Park, Penrith, 2750.

STUTCHBURY: Information is sought about the two younger children of Charles O'Connor of Forest, Tasmania who were brought to Melbourne after the death of Charles' first wife by the Stutchbury family. Please contact Mrs Helen Butler, 3 Shelby Road, St Ives, 2075. Telephone (02) 4493542.

Interviews

As well as writing letters to relatives, arrange to visit them if possible. This is an important way of gathering information, particularly from older relatives who may have valuable facts and anecdotes to pass on that they may be unable or unwilling to provide in letter form. If a family reunion is being contemplated, visiting is also an excellent way of re-establishing contact with distant or not so distant family members.

When interviewing relatives:

- use a cassette recorder where possible, if it does not offend

- photocopy the written record of interview form, included in this chapter (see Form F), and keep a written record of interview

- take along a copy of Table 1 which, as you will remember, lists the types of home source available, and ask your relatives if they have any of the items. Obtain photocopies of documents and photograph relevant possessions, if possible.

Again, record each source of information on your home sources form and the information itself on your pedigree charts and family data sheets. Do not forget to record the source of each item of information in the sections provided on the charts and sheets.

Form F: Written record of interview

Person interviewed _____

Address where interview took place _____

_____ Telephone number _____

Date _____

Additional notes	Record of interview

Family reunions

Another excellent way of collecting information about the family is to hold a family reunion. If the family is enthusiastic, this can become a regular event, with members getting together to share life stories, experiences, pedigrees and other information.

When arranging a family reunion:

- organise it well in advance to give relatives every chance to attend

- where possible, and especially if it is the first reunion, organise the occasion around a particular family event, such as a member turning 100 or a business or property reaching a certain age

- contact as many family members as you can and advertise the gathering in genealogical journals and local papers to catch the attention of relatives who are unknown or have been overlooked.

3

Using the records of libraries, genealogical societies and other organisations

What records do libraries, genealogical societies and other organisations have?
Having exhausted the resources of home and family, it is now time to check outside sources of information. This chapter will discuss the different institutions that can help you and the kinds of sources that you will find useful. Once you know where you need to go and what sources you need to use you can proceed with your research, using the research log provided, which is explained at the end of the chapter.

Local, State and special libraries, such as those of the genealogical societies, have research directories and other materials which will provide you with information about previous family research. You may find that someone else has already done work on the family you are interested in, so it is important to check first to avoid duplicating research.

Information about original documents is also provided by some libraries, allowing you to obtain, for example, such necessary details as the registration numbers of birth, death and marriage certificates before you apply for the documents themselves (thereby usually decreasing the cost involved). Note that birth entries do not get into indexes of births, deaths and marriages until approximately eighty years after the event to protect people still living.

Sources available in State and municipal libraries

Table 2 summarises the kinds of source usually available in your local or State library. It also summarises the content of such sources and provides a guide to their location. The abbreviations for Australian State and municipal libraries, which the libraries themselves use and which you will often see reference to, are used in Table 2 and explained in Table 3. In Chapter 8 you will find the addresses of the State and municipal libraries referred to in Table 2, plus those of other municipal libraries with genealogical holdings.

Keep the following points in mind when using Table 2.

- It mainly emphasises records available in libraries in the capital city of each State.

- It is only a very general summary of what and where information may be obtained. Additional sources of information are listed and discussed in Further Reading.

- It is arranged so that sources are listed in order of priority. You will need to check previous research first, hence research directories are mentioned first. Then you will need information about the most important original documents – birth, death and marriage certificates – in order to get copies, therefore indexes to births, deaths and marriages come next. After these, the works mentioned are the sources you are most likely to use, such as directories and occupational lists, and the more general sources of information you would use if writing a family history at a later date. As *Tracing Your Family History* deals mainly with research in Australia, the emphasis is on Australian sources. Therefore sources that you will need, if you decide to follow up convicts or free settlers emigrating to Australia, are listed at the end of Table 2, just before parish records, which take you into overseas research.

- Local municipal libraries are likely to have the records mentioned, but whether they do depends on their size, location and available funds.

- Certain municipal libraries are specifically mentioned because they specialise in genealogical material.

Table 2: Sources in State and municipal libraries

Source	Purpose and location
Research directories, e.g. *Genealogical Research Directory: National and Overseas, 1987* (see 'Research directories', Further Reading)	Show whether anyone has done research on a particular family or person before. They are also published by many genealogical societies on an irregular basis (see 'Members' interests lists', Table 5). **Location** All State libraries and most municipal libraries.
Indexes to births, deaths and marriages (BDM) (see 'Indexes to births, deaths and marriages', Further Reading)	Index certificates of registration (i.e. births, marriages and deaths) and surviving church records, and enable registration numbers to be obtained for purpose of obtaining copies of birth, death or marriage certificates. (NT Registrar of Births, Deaths and Marriages and SA Principal Registrar hold indexes for NT; the latter holds indexes for SA also.) **Location** ACT ANL NSW State and municipal libraries Qld QJO, QSL Tas. TSL, TMRL Vic. VCAU, VKEW, VSL WA WJSB, WLB

continued

Table 2 continued

Source	Purpose and location
Directories, e.g. almanacks, post office and telephone directories (see 'General directories', Further Reading) State and federal directories Overseas directories, mostly for British Isles	Give alphabetical lists of householders' names and addresses. Trades and professions often separately listed. Inhabitants of a particular town, suburb or street often given. Note that they can be two years out of date either way, i.e. a family may have moved in or out of an area without it being yet recorded in the directory. **Location** All State libraries and most municipal libraries. **Location** State libraries.
Source books, e.g. Frances Brown et al., *Family and Local History Sources in Victoria* (see 'Sources guides', Further Reading)	Discuss sources that may supply missing details. **Location** All State libraries and most municipal libraries.
How-to-do-it books (see 'General primary and secondary works', Further Reading)	Offer advice and variations on conducting research. **Location** All State libraries and most municipal libraries.
Occupational listings, e.g. *Biographical Register of the Victorian Parliament 1900– 1984, Dictionary of Australian Bushrangers* (see 'Biographical dictionaries', Further Reading)	List people by occupation, e.g. public servants, dentists, doctors. Occupational listings are found in directories discussed above, but there are also many special occupational listings for people in politics, medicine, law, the churches, government, etc. **Location** All State libraries and some municipal libraries.
Electoral rolls	Usually contain details of surname, given name, sex, residential address and occupation or profession for residents in Australia aged 21 years and over or, more recently, 18 years and over. **Location** Current electoral rolls and early electoral rolls are held by State libraries and most major municipal libraries. Also found in chief electoral offices in each State.
Monumental inscriptions and epitaphs	Give as much as name, date and place of death and burial, date and place of birth, and names of spouse, children and parents. May sometimes be only surviving record of these details. (Note that monumental inscriptions and epitaphs have been transcribed by members of many genealogical societies, and lists are often found in their libraries and magazines.) Some lists have been published in book or pamphlet form (see 'General primary and secondary works', Further Reading). **Location** NSW NML SA SSL WA WJSB

continued

Table 2 continued

Source	Purpose and location
Australian Joint Copying Project (AJCP)	Contains records relating to Australia held in the British Isles. Microfilm includes official documents, letters, maps, etc. held in county record offices, libraries, museums, and private collections. Information covers details of exploration, settlement and government of Australia, New Zealand and the Pacific region. Also includes information on missionary organisations, land and trading companies, learned societies and institutions and the activities of individuals from politicians and governors to small farmers, emigrants and convicts. As well, contains many reels of pictorial matter, e.g. rare maps and charts, sketches of early colonial buildings, detailed illustrations of plant and bird life and portraits of Aborigines. **Location** ACT ANL Vic. VSL (incomplete)
History and meanings of personal names and surnames	Useful for checking spellings of surnames and variations, particularly if you are having difficulty tracing someone in records such as indexes to births, deaths and marriages, as there can be many variations of the one surname. **Location** State libraries and most municipal libraries.
Family histories and biographies	Give dates, occupations, information about branches of a family which may be related to the one you are researching. Also useful to look at before writing your own family history to get ideas about approach, layout, etc. (Historical societies, as well as libraries, may hold these.) **Location** State libraries and some municipal libraries.
Newspapers	Obituaries, births, marriages and deaths notices, photographs, stories of interest, advertisements, correspondence and reports of public meetings all contain invaluable information about local and business activities. They all give you first-hand accounts of what life was like at the time of your ancestors. *Newspapers in Australian Libraries* lists newspapers held in ANL and other Australian libraries. **Location** All State libraries and many municipal libraries.
Maps	To check area where person lived in order to use a source, e.g. *International Genealogical Index*, you may need to know approximately where a person was born. Parish maps for the British Isles may be held by museums and historical societies, as well as some libraries. Maps recording who received colonial and State land from the Crown, either by grant or purchase, are available at these locations also and at your State department of lands. **Location** State Libraries and some municipal libraries.

continued

Table 2 continued

Source	Purpose and location
Local histories	Provide general information about a particular locality and its people, events, etc. Particularly useful when writing your family history for 'setting the scene' in which your ancestors lived. (Historical societies, as well as libraries, may hold these.) **Location** All State libraries and municipal libraries.
Dictionaries of biography, e.g. *Australian Dictionary of Biography, Who's Who in Australia* (see 'Biographical dictionaries', Further Reading)	Give details of better-known people, as well as small biographies of business people, farmers and settlers. Often the early volumes of biographies give date of arrival and places of origin because many entries were supplied by the family. **Location** State libraries and municipal libraries.
General histories, e.g. *Australian Encyclopaedia*	Fill in the details of the period in which an ancestor lived. (Historical societies, as well as libraries, may hold these.) **Location** State libraries and municipal libraries.
Shipping indexes	Give information on and photographs of ships. Some may list cabin passengers as given in newspapers, but these are not passenger lists. Passenger lists are kept at State archives offices, including Vic. Public Records Office (see Chapter 9). **Location** NSW NSL Qld QJO, QSL Vic. VSL WA WJSB
Convict records (see 'General directories', Further Reading)	Give names, dates of arrival, ages, places and dates of trial, physical descriptions, educated pardons, tickets of leave, certificates of freedom, depending on item. Many convict records are held at archives offices in each State, including Vic. Public Records Office. Many British Public Records Office records have been microfilmed and copies are held by various Australian libraries. **Location** NSW NML Qld QJO Tas. TSL WA WJSB
Parish records, mostly for British Isles	May provide as much information as names, dates, parentage, residence, age, occupation, family relationships, place and date of birth, but this depends on the record keeper. Usually give information about names, dates and parentage only. **Location** Most State libraries.

Table 3: Abbreviations for State and municipal libraries

All abbreviations used, except TMRL, VCAU and VKEW, are taken from the *National Union Catalogue of Australia* and are the symbols used by libraries. Only libraries referred to in the tables have been listed.

Australian Capital Territory
ANL   National Library of Australia

New South Wales
NML   Mitchell Library (part of State Library of New South Wales)
NSL   State Library of New South Wales

Queensland
QJO   John Oxley Library (part of Public Library of Queensland)
QSL   Public Library of Queensland

South Australia
SSL   State Library of South Australia

Tasmania
TMRL   Mersey Regional Library
TSL   State Library of Tasmania

Victoria
VCAU   Caulfield Library Service
VKEW   Kew Municipal Library
VSL   State Library of Victoria

Western Australia
WJSB   J. S. Battye Library of Western Australian History (part of State Library Board of Western Australia)
WLB   State Library Board of Western Australia

Government archive and department sources

Many sources of information are to be found outside libraries in such places as government archives and lands departments. Table 4 lists such sources and describes their uses and locations. Some sources listed in Table 2 are also listed in Table 4, if they are found both within and without State and municipal libraries. In Chapter 9 you will find the addresses of the places mentioned in Table 4.

Table 4: Sources in government archives and departments

Source	Purpose and location
Shipping indexes	For description of, see Table 2. **Location** State archives offices, including Vic. Public Records Office.
Passenger lists	May include name, age, marital status, place of origin, port of embarkation, religion and possibly occupation (quite often only 'lady' or 'gentleman' after 1900). **Location** ACT Archives Office (see also NSW Archives Office) NSW Archives Office NT Archives Office Qld Archives Office (see also NSW Archives Office) SA Archives Office Tas. Archives Office Vic. Public Records Office (see also NSW Archives Office) WA Archives Office

continued

Table 4 continued

Source	Purpose and location
Convict records	For description of, see Table 2. **Location** State archives offices, including Vic. Public Records Office.
Naturalisation papers	Give name, current and previous address, age and occupation, length of residence in Australia. Actual records held at the Australian Archives, Canberra. Index to Naturalisation Certificates gives only name, date and naturalisation number. **Location of Index to Naturalisation Certificates** ACT Archives Office (see also NSW Archives Office) NSW Archives Office NT ACT Archives Office Qld Archives Office (see also NSW Archives Office) SA Archives Office Tas. Archives Office, Supreme Court (see Supreme Court Register) Vic. Public Records Office (see also NSW Archives Office) WA Supreme Court (also WJSB)

Land records	Give names of parties involved, addresses, prices paid and improvements. Sometimes additional information, such as occupation and family relationships over a number of generations, is given.
	Location
	ACT Land Titles Office
	NSW Archives Office
	    Registry of Land Titles and Deeds
	NT Department of Law
	Qld Archives Office
	    Department of Mapping and Surveying
	    Lands Department
	    Titles Office
	SA Archives Office
	    General Registry Office
	    Land Office
	    Lands Titles Office
	Tas. Archives Office
	    Deeds Office
	    Land Titles and Deeds Office
	Vic. Department of Conservation, Forests and Lands
	    Public Record Office (Laverton)
	    Registrar of Titles
	    Registrar-General's Office
	WA Office of Titles (also WJSB)

continued

Table 4 continued

Source	Purpose and location
Inquest reports	Give type of death, name and age of deceased, number in register, date and locality of death, details and value of property owned at the time and outcome of the inquest. **Location** State archives offices, including Vic. Public Record Office.
Military documents	Give name, date and place of birth, enlistment, discharge, etc., but usually only for officers. *Roll Call* gives Australian War Memorial holdings (see 'Sources guides', Further Reading). **Location** ACT Australian War Memorial State military establishments, e.g. Victoria Barracks, Vic., hold military histories.

Probate records, wills, etc.	Give name of deceased, residence, occupation (in some cases), date of death and value of estate. Can also provide invaluable information, such as names of spouse and children of the deceased as well as grandparents, parents and other family members. Birthplace and possessions, e.g. land, houses and family heirlooms, such as portraits, etc., are often also mentioned.
	Location
	ACT Registrar of Probates
	NSW Archives Office
	    Supreme Court of NSW
	    (also Society of Australian Genealogists)
	NT Registrar of Probates
	Qld Archives Office
	SA Archives Office
	    Probate Registry
	Tas. Probate Registry
	    Supreme Court of NSW
	Vic. Registrar of Probates
	    Supreme Court of NSW
	WA Probate Office
	    Public Trust Office

Genealogical societies' sources

You will find that genealogical societies and their libraries can greatly help you with your research. You will probably want to join a society, but you do not have to become a member to use the library, although you may have to pay a user's fee. In general the aims of genealogical societies are to:

- promote genealogical and family history research

- promote the preservation of historical records and personal records

- further the study of genealogy by the collection of historical data

- educate people in genealogical and family history methods

- publish booklets, magazines and so on to promote genealogy and family history

- provide a limited research service for 'out of town' members and to advise on research problems

- organise meetings and field days for the exchange of information

- provide a library service

- maintain lists of members' particular family history interests.

Genealogical societies fall into two categories: general genealogical societies and the Church of Jesus Christ of Latter-day Saints Genealogical Department (formerly the Genealogical Society of Utah). You will find details of the names, addresses, interests, publications and services of both the general genealogical societies and the Church of Jesus Christ of Latter-day Saints in Chapter 10.

The libraries of genealogical societies are invaluable repositories of the sources listed in Table 5. Many of the genealogical societies' libraries also contain a variety of research aids, such as:

- indexes of births, deaths and marriages for all Australian States

- post office directories

- shipping records

- research directories

- maps

- government gazettes and armed services information

- cemetery indexes.

Table 5: Sources in genealogical societies' libraries

Source	Purpose
International Genealogical Index (IGI)	On microfiche. Gives information, extracted from the original documents, about names of parents and spouse and dates and locations of births, christenings, marriages and other events. It lists over 90 million deceased persons from every country in the world and includes people born at sea. Covers period before 1870 (before 1538, for England). Indexed under country and place of event.
Family Group Records Collection	Information on families all over the world submitted by people in the Church of Jesus Christ of Latter-day Saints. (Available at Church libraries only.)
Members' interests lists	Contain many surnames, places and dates relating to families being researched and include name and address of interested society member. May appear as card systems, microfiche or published booklets.
Family histories	Either partly researched or fully written up.
Genealogical magazines	Record current research, answer questions on research, contain articles on genealogy and reviews of the latest books on genealogy. You can advertise research requests.
Monumental inscriptions	For description of, see Table 2.

Recording your findings

Now that you know what sources will be useful and where to go, you are ready to further your research. The research log provided in this chapter (see Form G) will enable you to:

- list the questions and details you wish to research

- list records you have researched – both successfully and unsuccessfully – and all information found in these, to avoid accidentally duplicating your work and the problem of many 'bits of paper'

- record genealogical information needed for pedigree charts, for example.

Filling in the research log

[1] Photocopy Form G for your use – if you require more space for your findings, make more than one photocopy.

[2] As a guide, use the filled-in sample of a research log provided (see Figure 12). Note that correct titles and Caulfield Library reference numbers have been given for Victorian indexes and directories, but microfiche and page numbers and the 'Results of research' findings are fictitious.

Many sources of information, such as indexes to births, deaths and marriages, are now recorded on microfiche. You will find the microfiche reader easy and convenient to use.

3 In the space provided on Form G write in the questions and details you wish to research (for example, in Figure 12, Q1 refers to checking what previous work has been done on the Sagar family). Note that the questions will be progressive: that is, as you answer one question another will arise, which in turn will lead to a further question and so on.

4 Using the columns provided, fully document each record you look up: by noting the date you worked on it, the place where it is held, its call number or other identifying information and its page or microfiche number; and by describing its nature, that is, whether it is a book, film or some other kind of record.

5 Make sure you record the works you have searched unsuccessfully, as well as those in which you have found information.

6 Note your findings in the 'Results of research' column. Transfer all the information you have gained to the appropriate forms, such as the pedigree chart – having to fill out the 'information transferred' column will remind you to do this. For example, Samuel James Sagar's birth date and place noted on the filled-in sample (see Figure 12) would be transferred to the Sagar family's pedigree chart. Much of your information will be transferred to the ancestor research sheet (Form H), if you are interested in the history of a particular ancestor (see Chapter 5).

Form G: Research log

Questions and details to be researched

Date of research	Name of library, government office, etc.	Library call number, collection number, etc.	Type of record and particulars	Page or microfiche number, certificate registration number	Results of research	Name of form to which information transferred	Legibility

Figure 12: Sample research log (Form G)

Questions and details to be researched

1 Any research done on Sagar family previously? Any Sagar family members found in Victoria?

2 Date Samuel James Sagar born? (Family thinks 1870s in Victoria.)

3 Did Samuel have other brothers and sisters?

4 When were Samuel Sagar's parents married? Samuel born 1876, so try before that year.

5 What did Benjamin Sagar do? May have lived first at Ballarat? Where is CHl. or Chil.? Where did Benjamin settle?

Date of research	Name of library, government office, etc.	Library call number, collection number, etc.	Type of record and particulars	Page or microfiche number, certificate registration number	Results of research	Name of form to which information transferred	Legibility
Q1	Caulfield	Ref.	Book:	p.453	Entry: Sagar; c.1870; Ballarat, Vic.; researcher no.5413-		
10April 1988	Library	929.1	Genealogical Research Directory, 1987		index shows this is Mrs A. Peterson and gives address. 11 Apr. 1988 letter requesting information sent to Mrs Peterson.		
Q2	Caulfield	Ref.	Microfiche:		1870 - 1875 ×		
21April 1988	Library	929.3945	Index to Births 1/7/1853 - 31/12/1895	Fiche 48, p.283	Entry 1876: Sagar, Samuel James; registration no.14588; father Benjamin, mother Marr, Eleanor; place CHl. 1877-1878× 1880-1881× 1883-1892×	Pedigree charts 1&2 Family data sheet 2	Mother's name blurred
Q3	Caulfield	Ref.	Microfiche:				
23April 1988	Library	929.3945	Index to Births 1/7/1853 - 31/12/1895	Fiche 51, p.291	Entry 1879: Sagar, Elsie May; reg.no.14456; father Benjamin; mother Mann, Eleanor; place Chil.		
				Fiche 72, p.326	Entry 1882: Sagar, Edward; reg.no.25670; father Benjamin, mother Marr, Eleanor; place Chil.		

Date	Place	Ref.	Source	Fiche ref.	Findings	Recorded on
					Note: Mother's maiden name misspelt (Marr then Mann) & different ways of recording same place (Chl. and Chil.)	
Q4 23 April 1988	Caulfield Library	929.3945	Microfiche: Index to Marriages 1/7/1853 – 31/12/1895	Fiche 102, p.104	Entry 1874: Sagar, Benjamin; reg. no. 345; married Marr, Eleanor. Note: Surname misspelt (Sagur not Sagar).	Pedigree chart 2 Surname blurred
Q5 23 April 1988	Caulfield Library	910.3	Microfiche: Baillière's Victorian Gazetteers, 1865, 1870, 1879	Fiche 5, p.105	Place names 1870 starting with Chil. were: Chilburragon, Mt.– no mention of people living here Childer's Cove — no mention of people living here Chillington Station – Nth Gipps., occupiers Buckley & Mason Chiltern — near Rutherglen and Albury, population 2200 Chilwell — see Newtown-Chilwell.	
				Fiche 6, p.220	Newtown-Chilwell — a Geelong suburb, population 5000. Chiltern or Chilwell most likely. Try Chilwell c.1876.	
5 June 1988	Caulfield Library	929.3945	Microfiche: Port Phillip / Victoria Directories 1839–1900		No records 1876, so try 1875. No record of Sagars at Chilwell. Therefore check Chiltern.	Family data sheet 2
			Section "Official post office directory of Victoria 1868–1881"	Fiche 6, p.482	Entry 1875: Sagar, Benjamin; wheelwright; Chiltern.	
			Section "Trades and professions"	Fiche 2, p.232	Entry "Wheelwrights": Sagar, Benjamin; Main St, Chiltern.	
			Section "1880s directory"	Fiche 6, p.496	Entry: Sagar, Benjamin; wheelwright; Newtown.	
			Section "Wise's"	Fiche 7, p.526	Entry: Sagar, Benjamin; wheelwright; Newtown. Entry: Sagar, Mrs.; Bank St, Newtown.	
			Victoria post office directory 1884–1900?			

[7] If a record, such as a microfiche, is difficult to read because it is, for example, blurred, note this in the 'Legibility' column. If any doubts about the accuracy of the findings arise, a note that the record was illegible will alert you to the possibility that a mistake has resulted, and you can double-check your information.

Problems associated with using records

A number of difficulties can arise when you are looking up records. Keeping the problems in mind as you undertake your research will enable you to deal with them in the most efficient way and allow you to avoid unnecessary 'dead end' research. There are books which deal specifically with problems in genealogy and their solutions (see 'Guides to genealogy' in Further Reading), so only the more general difficulties are summarised here.

- There can be several spellings of the same name. 'Sagar', for example, may appear as 'Sager' or Sagur'. Such variations may represent legitimate alternative spellings of the same name – or they may be the result of erroneous recording on the original documents. For instance, the marriage certificate of the parents of Louisa Gelme (born 1858) and Louisa's own marriage certificate give the surname as 'Gelme', yet there is no record of birth under this name. On checking further back in the alphabetically listed records for 1858, all relevant details are found entered under the incorrect spelling 'Geline'.

  Therefore check alternative spellings in name books and, when looking up records, such as microfiche, try different spellings of the same name, particularly when you are fairly certain that records should exist because, for example, the name you are looking for appears on another certificate.

- Details of dates, places and names are not always correctly recorded. As well, some records are incomplete. It is often necessary to verify details, particularly on death certificates, by checking other entries, such as those in birth, marriage and even cemetery records.

- Records may be difficult to read because of the ravages of time. They may be damaged by inadequate storage, fire or water. Or they may be difficult to decipher on microfiche because of the poor handwriting of the official registering the event. In any of these cases, seek alternative records.

- Secondary sources of information, such as works by modern historians, will never be as accurate as those recorded at the time of the event, that is, primary sources. This is another reason why it is important to note the source of your information as you progress: you may need to verify the information of a secondary source you have used.

- Many people changed their names on arrival in Australia. Hopefully, there will be some indication of this change in family records.

4

Obtaining certificates

How do I obtain the records I want?
To this point in your search for the most important primary documents – birth, death and marriage certificates – you have:

1. checked what certificates your family does and does not possess

2. established what information you still require, just as in our example we recorded that we wanted to find out when in the 1870s Samuel James Sagar had been born (see Figure 12)

3. consulted indexes of births, deaths and marriages in a library to establish the date of the event in which you are interested (in our example we established that Samuel James Sagar had been born in the year 1876)

4. recorded the registration number of the certificate provided by an index of births, deaths and marriages, as well as the year of the event, in your research log. Samuel James Sagar's birth certificate registration number was given as 14588. (Remember that, although it is not essential to provide the number when you are applying to a State registry for a certificate, the cost is usually cut by almost half if you do so.)

So you are now ready to complete your task by obtaining the certificate that will provide you with the full details you require. The final steps are:

5. pick up the relevant application form at your local post office or State registry: there are separate forms for birth, death and marriage certificates (see Figure 13 for an example of an application form for a birth certificate) and a separate form must be used for each person

Figure 13: Application form for a birth extract or certificate

PLEASE USE BLOCK LETTERS

APPLICATION FOR EXTRACT OR CERTIFICATE OF

BIRTHS IN VICTORIA

Registration of Births, Deaths & Marriages Regulations Form 4

THIS RECEIPT MUST BE PRODUCED WHEN COLLECTING DOCUMENTS

Applications to be made to:

Registry of Births, Deaths & Marriages
P.O. Box 4332
Melbourne 3001

or delivered to

295 Queen Street
Melbourne
Telephone: 603 5900

Insert family name and initials of the birth		Year of birth	
			Received amount printed by cash register

TICK APPROPRIATE BOXES

☐ Full certificate $21 If official Entry No. **NOT QUOTED**

                            $10.50 If official Entry No. **IS QUOTED**

☐ Extract $10.50

☐ Priority Service $19.00
   (Additional Fee)

☐ Post (complete section below)   **FEES (Effective from 1.11.87 to 31.10.88)**

☐ Collect   **Reviewed Annually**

Enclosed is a cheque/money order/cash

for $...........................

DETAILS OF BIRTH REQUIRED

Official Entry No. If Known			Place of birth City/suburb/town	VICTORIA	
Date of birth	Day /	Month /	Year	Or years to be searched 5 year period(s)	From.. to..
Family name (at birth)			Christian or given names		
Fathers name	Family name			Christian or given names	
Mothers name	Family name (Maiden)			Christian or given names	

APPLICANTS DETAILS

Applicants name		Signature of applicant	
Applicants address			Tel:
Reason document is required		Relationship of applicant	

Office hours for making applications—8.30 a.m. to 4 p.m. Monday to Friday

IF THIS APPLICATION RELATES TO A LIVING PERSON OTHER THAN YOURSELF **WRITTEN AUTHORITY** MAY BE REQUIRED

PLEASE COMPLETE THIS SECTION IF DOCUMENT IS TO BE POSTED
PLEASE USE BLOCK LETTERS

Name	
Address and Postcode	

6 fill out all the details you can on this form

7 decide whether you wish to apply for an extract or a certificate: an extract (see Figure 14) usually mentions only the name of the party, the date and place of the event and the registration number (this will usually not be enough information for your purposes); a certificate (see Figure 15) provides all the details appearing on the original registered entry and, in fact, is now a photocopy of the original

8 send the application form to the Registry of Births, Deaths and Marriages in the capital city of your State. You will find the addresses of all the State registries and details of current charges in Chapter 11 (but check costs before applying).

Figure 14: Extract of birth entry

STATE OF VICTORIA

EXTRACT OF BIRTH ENTRY

Registration Number

18926/83

Date of birth   **15 April 1983**

Place of birth   **East Melbourne**

Name

                Janneke Anne FITZGERALD

Sex

                Female

Issued at Melbourne

GOVERNMENT STATIST

This extract of entry is forwarded as confirmation that the birth has been registered in the records of this office.

The extract should be retained as it will be acceptable as proof of age for school attendance, employment, insurance purposes, &c., within Australia.

A certified copy of the complete entry may be obtained on payment of a fee of $8·00 if the registration number is quoted. If this number is not quoted, the fee will be $16·00

APPLICATION SHOULD BE MADE TO THE GOVERNMENT STATIST. 295, QUEEN STREET, MELBOURNE, VICTORIA, 3000

Figure 15: Certificate of birth entry

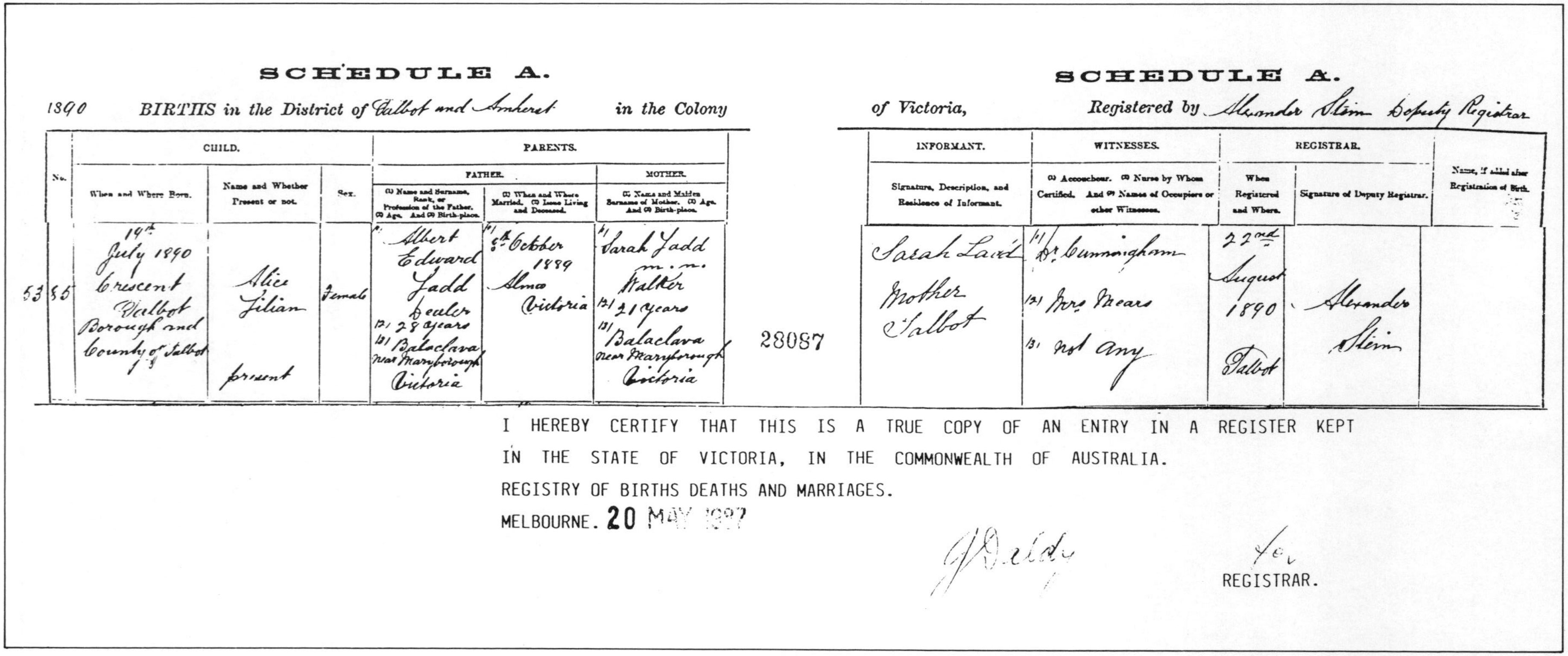

SCHEDULE A. SCHEDULE A.

1890 BIRTHS in the District of Talbot and Amherst in the Colony of Victoria, Registered by Alexander Stein Deputy Registrar

No.	CHILD. When and Where Born.	CHILD. Name and Whether Present or not.	CHILD. Sex.	PARENTS. FATHER. (1) Name and Surname, Rank, or Profession of the Father. (2) Age. And (3) Birth-place.	PARENTS. FATHER. (1) When and Where Married. (2) Issue Living and Deceased.	PARENTS. MOTHER. (1) Name and Maiden Surname of Mother. (2) Age. And (3) Birth-place.	INFORMANT. Signature, Description, and Residence of Informant.	WITNESSES. (1) Accoucheur. (2) Nurse by Whom Certified. And (3) Names of Occupiers or other Witnesses.	REGISTRAR. When Registered and Where.	REGISTRAR. Signature of Deputy Registrar.	Name, if added after Registration of Birth.
5385	19th July 1890 Crescent Talbot Borough and County of Talbot	Alice Lilian present	Female	(1) Albert Edward Ladd Dealer (2) 28 years (3) Balaclava near Maryborough Victoria	(1) 5th October 1889 Alma Victoria	(1) Sarah Ladd m.n. Walker (2) 21 years (3) Balaclava near Maryborough Victoria	Sarah Ladd Mother Talbot	(1) Dr Cunningham (2) Mrs Mears (3) not any	22nd August 1890 Talbot	Alexander Stein	

28087

I HEREBY CERTIFY THAT THIS IS A TRUE COPY OF AN ENTRY IN A REGISTER KEPT IN THE STATE OF VICTORIA, IN THE COMMONWEALTH OF AUSTRALIA.

REGISTRY OF BIRTHS DEATHS AND MARRIAGES.

MELBOURNE. 20 MAY 1987

for REGISTRAR.

Points to remember when you are seeking certificates

- When looking up births in indexes to births, deaths and marriages, be aware of two additional categories that may appear at the end of the alphabetical listing (that is, after Z) on any one microfiche: 'Marine births', which alphabetically lists those born at sea, and 'Unknowns', which concerns children born without a name officially being given to them – for example, an entry may appear as 'Unknown, female, born 1835, New.' and in a variety of other ways.

- The details that appear on a certificate will vary from State to State and from period to period: *Birth, Death and Marriage Certificates in Australia*, by Faye Young and Don Harris, gives in table form the details that appear on certificates in each State at different times.

- Be prepared for several weeks' delay in the processing of your application, because registries are handling an increasing volume of work as genealogy becomes more popular.

- The majority of births, deaths and marriages were registered when official registration commenced in the different Australian colonies, but many events were not recorded or were recorded incorrectly. Some events were not registered because they occurred in remote districts, or their details were not forwarded to the registrar or were lost in transit. Sometimes a surname was spelt incorrectly because the recorder had difficulty understanding regional accents or foreign names or could not spell. As well, standards of handwriting varied considerably and some early registrations are almost indecipherable.

Completing your charts and sheets

Where do I go from here?
Having checked the records both at home and in libraries, obtained certificates and filled in gaps on your forms, you need to ask yourself the following questions.

1. Have I filled in all the details on my pedigree charts to my satisfaction? Are there any further branches of the family I wish to trace? Do I want to supplement my written charts with a photograph pedigree chart (see Form A)?

2. Have I got all the details I require on my family data sheets? Are there any other couples for whom I want to do family data sheets?

If you are satisfied that you have done as much as you want to on your pedigree charts and family data sheets you are now ready to follow up a particular ancestor in greater detail and perhaps write your family's history.

5

Following up one ancestor

What do I want to learn about my family?
Having spent some time by now researching your family, you may find that
one person stands out as particularly colourful or interesting. Perhaps you have
discovered someone who:

- had interesting reasons for emigrating to Australia

- led a very adventurous or infamous life

- started a business or a farm

- was employed in an occupation, craft or profession of historical interest: for
  example, as a housemaid or blacksmith

- invented something unique

- was part of a major event in Australia, such as the gold rushes

- showed particular strength of character: for example, a matriarch who raised
  six children and ran the family business as well, after her husband died.

Sometimes, of course, you will be interested in an ancestor simply because you
have discovered a lot of information about that person, which makes him or her
come alive.

So your aim now will be to 'record information about one member of my
family'. To accomplish this you need to work again through the remaining five
basic questions.

Recording on the ancestor research sheet

What do I already know about my family and how do I record it?
In this case the question becomes 'What do I already know about the ancestor I am interested in and how do I record it?'.

An ancestor research sheet (Form H) is given in this chapter to enable you to record in one place information on the particular ancestor you have chosen. It allows you to record in detail the background of an ancestor and has provision for information about education, qualifications, places of residence, member-ships, occupations and so on. It also provides spaces for the names of the ancestor's parents and for details of the spouse and children. Note that many spaces have been left for children as large families were not uncommon in early days.

Filling in the ancestor research sheet

1 Photocopy Form H for your use.

2 As a guide, use the filled-in sample of an ancestor research sheet (Figure 16), which continues our example of Samuel James Sagar.

3 On Form H fill in all the details you already have, that is, the information from your pedigree charts and family data sheets and from your prior knowledge. Also add details contained in home and family sources after you have explored the family possessions (see following discussion).

4 Use the right-hand column, 'For further details see', in the section allotted to your ancestor's children, to refer to any pedigree charts or family data sheets where information is given in greater detail.

Using home and family sources further

What information do I have at home?
Check the home sources form (Form E) that you have previously filled in to see whether the name of your ancestor is mentioned, for example, in letters. There is no need to look at birth, death and marriage certificates, as you have already checked them and recorded your findings on your pedigree charts and family data sheets.

Next, check your home sources more carefully because, although you have noted them on your home sources form, you will not know in detail what the sources, such as the family Bible, contain. As you do this, you may find it useful to list the relevant items and to briefly indicate their contents on a home sources card for later reference. (See the discussion on 'Organising home sources information on cards', Chapter 6, and Figure 19 which demonstrates how a home sources card is developed for Samuel James Sagar.) Finally, record the facts you discover from your close examination of home sources on your ancestor research sheet.

Form H: Ancestor research sheet

Surname _____

Forenames _____

Is there a photograph available? _____

	Day	Month	Year	City, town, place	State	Country
Birth						
Baptism						
Marriage						
Death						
Burial						

Places of residence

Education (schools, etc.)	Church affiliations

Qualifications (professional, apprenticeship, etc.)

Memberships (professional bodies, societies, etc.)

Continued

Occupations

Military service (rank, areas of service, dates, decorations)

Hobbies, pastimes

Other details of interest

Father's name	Mother's name

Spouse's name

Spouse's life events	Day	Month	Year	City, town, place	State	Country
Birth						
Baptism						
Marriage						
Death						
Burial						

Continued

Children (in order of birth)	Place	Date	For further details see
1 _____			
Born	_____	_____	_____
Married to _____	_____	_____	_____
Died	_____	_____	_____
2 _____			
Born	_____	_____	_____
Married to _____	_____	_____	_____
Died	_____	_____	_____
3 _____			
Born	_____	_____	_____
Married to _____	_____	_____	_____
Died	_____	_____	_____
4 _____			
Born	_____	_____	_____
Married to _____	_____	_____	_____
Died	_____	_____	_____
5 _____			
Born	_____	_____	_____
Married to _____	_____	_____	_____
Died	_____	_____	_____
6 _____			
Born	_____	_____	_____
Married to _____	_____	_____	_____
Died	_____	_____	_____
7 _____			
Born	_____	_____	_____
Married to _____	_____	_____	_____
Died	_____	_____	_____
8 _____			
Born	_____	_____	_____
Married to _____	_____	_____	_____
Died	_____	_____	_____
9 _____			
Born	_____	_____	_____
Married to _____	_____	_____	_____
Died	_____	_____	_____

Continued

Children (in order of birth)	Place	Date	For further details see
10 _____			
Born	_____	_____	_____
Married to _____	_____	_____	_____
Died	_____	_____	_____
11 _____			
Born	_____	_____	_____
Married to _____	_____	_____	_____
Died	_____	_____	_____
12 _____			
Born	_____	_____	_____
Married to _____	_____	_____	_____
Died	_____	_____	_____
13 _____			
Born	_____	_____	_____
Married to _____	_____	_____	_____
Died	_____	_____	_____
14 _____			
Born	_____	_____	_____
Married to _____	_____	_____	_____
Died	_____	_____	_____
15 _____			
Born	_____	_____	_____
Married to _____	_____	_____	_____
Died	_____	_____	_____
16 _____			
Born	_____	_____	_____
Married to _____	_____	_____	_____
Died	_____	_____	_____
17 _____			
Born	_____	_____	_____
Married to _____	_____	_____	_____
Died	_____	_____	_____
18 _____			
Born	_____	_____	_____
Married to _____	_____	_____	_____
Died	_____	_____	_____

Figure 16: Sample ancestor research sheet (Form H)

Surname _Sagar_

Forenames _Samuel James_

Is there a photograph available? _In family Bible (item 1), page 130_

	Day	Month	Year	City, town, place	State	Country
Birth	27	September	1876	Chiltern	Victoria	Australia
Baptism	30	September	1876	"	"	"
Marriage	1	March	1896	"	"	"
Death	5	June	1930	"	"	"
Burial	8	June	1930	"	"	"

Places of residence

Main Street, Chiltern, Victoria

Amy Street, Chiltern, Victoria

Education (schools, etc.)

Chiltern primary school

Church affiliations

Church of England

Qualifications (professional, apprenticeship, etc.)

Carpenter's certificate

Memberships (professional bodies, societies, etc.)

Church of England vestry

Chiltern Fire Brigade

Continued

Figure 16 continued

Occupations

Carpenter

Military service (rank, areas of service, dates, decorations)

Nil

Hobbies, pastimes

Horse-riding and going to the races
Shooting
Cards

Other details of interest

Saved a child from a burning hotel in the biggest local fire
Built churches and town halls in the district which are still standing

Father's name	Mother's name
Benjamin Sagar	Eleanor Marr

Spouse's name

Margaret May Seller

Spouse's life events	Day	Month	Year	City, town, place	State	Country
Birth	6	April	1878	Chiltern	Victoria	Australia
Baptism	10	April	1878	"	"	"
Marriage	1	March	1896	"	"	"
Death	5	May	1944	"	"	"
Burial	7	May	1944	"	"	"

Continued

Figure 16 continued

Children (in order of birth)	Place	Date	For further details see
1 <u>Harry Peter Sagar</u>			
Born	<u>Chiltern, Victoria</u>	<u>9 Mar. 1899</u>	
Married to <u>Josephine Taylor</u>	<u>Chiltern, Victoria</u>	<u>17 Feb. 1923</u>	<u>Pedigree</u>
Died	<u>Chiltern, Victoria</u>	<u>4 May 1945</u>	<u>Chart 1</u>
2 <u>Jane Sagar</u>			
Born	<u>Chiltern, Victoria</u>	<u>13 Jan. 1901</u>	
Married to _____	_____	_____	
Died	<u>Chiltern, Victoria</u>	<u>6 June 1929</u>	
3 <u>George Sagar</u>			
Born	<u>Chiltern, Victoria</u>	<u>7 July 1907</u>	
Married to <u>Eve Sarah Harris</u>	<u>Chiltern, Victoria</u>	<u>4 Apr. 1930</u>	
Died			

Note: if you are planning to write a family history later, you may also wish at this stage to record any details you find about other family members to avoid going through the same home items twice (again see the discussion of 'Organising home sources information on cards', Chapter 6).

Contacting relatives

Researching an ancestor provides another opportunity to contact family members for missing details by either writing letters or visiting. Using the sample letter given in Figure 9, Chapter 2, as a basis, write letters requesting further information on the ancestor you have chosen. Remember to number, record and file away the replies after you have transferred the relevant details to your ancestor research sheet.

Sources in libraries, genealogical societies and other organisations

What records do libraries, genealogical societies and other organisations have?
Using the research log (Form G) discussed in Chapter 3, write down the missing details you wish to research. Refer again to the filled-in sample of a research log (Figure 12) to see how to organise your research and to ensure that you make the best use of the research log.

Records in libraries and other bodies will help you 'put flesh on the bones' of the research you have already carried out and will give you a more rounded picture of your ancestor and the times in which he or she lived. Table 6 summarises the sources you could check. Tables 2, 4 and 5 in Chapter 3, as you will remember, outline in detail the holdings of the State and municipal libraries, government bodies and genealogical societies.

Table 6: Summary of sources of information

Information required	Possible research source
Occupation of person	Certificates, letters, trade directories, newspapers, professional listings
Residence	Postal directories, electoral rolls, Sands and McDougall's directories
General locality in which person resided	Local histories, newspapers
General life and times of ancestor	Biographies, general and local histories, letters

Using records: an example

To gain an idea of how to find out more about one person let's look at the example of Benjamin Sagar, in whom we have become interested because he is the father of Samuel James Sagar, the ancestor we are researching.

On the filled-in sample of a research log (Figure 12) we raise the question 'What did Benjamin Sagar do?' (see Q5). We already know from Samuel James Sagar's birth information that Samuel was born at a place with the abbreviation 'Chil.'. We will assume, although this will not always be the case, that his family, including Benjamin, also lived at 'Chil.' and proceed from there as follows.

1 To find out what place 'Chil.' is we might look up present Victorian place names. But a number of names have changed since the time of Samuel James Sagar.

2 A book called *Baillière's Victorian Gazetteers 1865, 1870, 1879* lists the place names in Victoria at those dates and also briefly describes the different localities. Looking up 'Chil.', we find a number of place names beginning with those letters (see the list recorded for Q5 in Figure 12). By a process of elimination we are left with Chilwell or Chiltern.

3 Now we look up the postal directories because they will give us occupations. We find nothing under Sagar for Chilwell.

4 We find in the alphabetical listing for Chiltern that Benjamin Sagar was a wheelwright there. Checking the trades and professionals section of the directory, we find under 'Wheelwrights' that he lived in Main Street, Chiltern.

5 Checking later postal directories we find that he moved to Newtown.

Obtaining records

How do I obtain records I want?
Remember to obtain any registration certificates outstanding for your particular ancestor (see Chapter 4). Again, first check to see if the registration number of the certificate you want appears in an index to births, deaths and marriages (see Chapter 3), before applying to your State registry. (Remember that birth entries do not get into indexes to births until approximately eighty years after the event.)

Using a professional genealogist

As you progress in your research you may find that you reach a dead-end because of difficulty in obtaining records, lack of expertise or insufficient time for research. Genealogical records may be inaccessible to you because of distance. Under these circumstances you may wish to hire a professional genealogist to do your searching for you or to do part of the research while you continue with the rest.

Whatever the reason, it is important to keep the following points in mind when engaging a professional genealogist:

- usually you will be paying the genealogist by the hour, so it is important to make your initial request for information very specific, and unless you give him or her all the relevant information a lot of time and money will be wasted

- it is important to engage a reputable genealogist who is suitably qualified: he or she should have a Diploma of Family Historical Studies or the equivalent (see Chapter 12 on how to obtain the names and addresses of suitable genealogists)

- check the schedule of fees with the genealogist because this varies

- remember that all genealogical research takes time, so do not expect an answer to your letter or request in a matter of weeks. It could be months if unexpected difficulties arise.

Usually you will make your request by letter. Keep in mind the points made in Chapter 2 about writing clear and concise letters. Use the sample letters provided (see Figures 17 and 18) when you are enquiring about and employing a professional genealogist. File copies of the letters you send and the replies.

Figure 17: Letter making enquiries to a professional genealogist

Name   *Date*
Address

Dear _____
I am at present engaged in researching my family tree and require the services of a genealogist. Please send me a schedule of your fees and an estimation of the time required to complete a typical search.

Thank you, in anticipation.

Yours sincerely

Figure 18: Letter requesting a genealogist's services

Name   *Date*
Address

Dear _____
I wish to engage you in helping me trace a particular branch of my family tree on the basis of the $— per hour you quoted me in your letter of _____.

I would like you to trace the father of Samuel James Sagar whose name is Benjamin Sagar. I want to know:

1 his date of birth
2 his parents' names and dates of birth, marriage and death.

Attached please find a pedigree chart of the Sagars which shows the extent of my research. I also include a copy of Benjamin's death certificate, which is the only certificate of his that I have in my possession.

Should I come across any further relevant information I will send it to you.

Thank you, in anticipation.

Yours sincerely

Adam Sagar
_____

Where do I go from here?
Having found the initial information you wanted on your particular ancestor, you will again want to ask yourself a few questions.

1. Have I collected all the information I want about his or her life and times?

2. Do I know what made this person unique and interesting in terms of interests, outlook on life and commitments?

3. Are there other ancestors that I now want to follow up in the same way: that is, do I want to start another ancestor research sheet?

4. Am I satisfied with my research to date and do I now wish to move on to writing a family history?

6

Writing your family history

What do I want to learn about my family?

As you progress in your exploration of the history of one ancestor and you experience the pleasure of getting to know intimately the life of that person, you will often find that you develop a strong desire to study other family members in the same depth. You may well become vitally interested in tracing the family's progress over many decades to discover how the lives of members changed from generation to generation. In this case, your answer to our basic question becomes 'To learn how my family fared over several generations, by writing a detailed family history'.

Writing a family history is also an excellent way of pulling your findings into a more coherent form. Merely collecting forms and charts that record dates and facts leaves your information still rather fragmented and inaccessible to others, whereas writing an account of the family makes your research much more interesting to yourself and your relatives. Your family history, in whatever final form it takes, will also be of interest to people engaged in historical or genealogical research and to future generations of your family as well.

Planning your history

Having decided to write your family history, you must then decide how you want to write it, that is, what approach you wish to take. You can write your family history in any of the ways outlined below. In all cases, although you may start with a central person (often the ancestor you have researched), you will go on to develop a number of 'leading characters'.

- You can write about yourself and then the family members leading up to yourself. This is not a common approach but can be very useful in terms of practising your writing skills. Alternatively, you can use this approach as a preliminary exercise before undertaking a larger history. It is much easier to start by writing about someone you know, that is, yourself. Your work will also provide a record of yourself and your times for your descendants.

- You can choose one ancestor (usually the first one to come out to Australia) and tell his or her story and then that of each generation of the family line from that time on.

- You can choose a recent ancestor and trace the family back from this person.

- You can choose a particularly interesting aspect of your family's history, such as the family's development of a successful business or an invention, and write about that.

What do I already know about my family and how do I record it?
Once you have decided on your approach, you need to check whether you have enough information to carry out the project. For example, do you have enough to be able to write a story about particular ancestors, including anecdotes about them, their thoughts and feelings and a detailed description of the general times in which they lived?

You already have your completed pedigree charts and family data sheets to provide you with basic information about the generations. And you have your findings about one ancestor, or perhaps several, most of which will already be recorded in an easily retrievable form. So it is time to check through and organise all your home sources more carefully.

What information do I have at home?
Family anecdotes and certain home sources, such as letters and photographs, will now be of importance, whereas initially basic documents, such as certificates, were of more use. You will find it very helpful to put the information you discover on cards, using a separate one for each family member.

Organising home sources information on cards

1 Buy yourself some 100 x 150 millimetre cards.

2 Taking a card for each member of the family, write the surname and given names in the top left-hand corner and the reference number of the family member (from your pedigree chart) in the top right-hand corner.

3 Record on the cards the information you gain from each home source plus the reference number you have already given that item on your home sources form.

4 As a guide, use the examples provided in Figures 19, 20 and 21.

5 File the cards, alphabetically by surname then forenames, in boxes. For example, Harry Gregory Sagar, Harry Peter Sagar and Samuel James Sagar will be filed in that order.

Taking the examples of Figures 19, 20 and 21, you can see that home sources cards are useful indicators of the family items that will provide the detailed information needed for a family history. The summaries of the three sources so far recorded on Samuel James Sagar's card (see Figure 19) suggest that we will be able to include a photograph of Samuel in any account of him, and that we will also be able to describe his interests, his style of living and something of the economic conditions of his time – that is, that we will perhaps find enough information in home sources to be able to make Samuel the central, or one of the central, characters in our fictitious history of the Sagar family (or, as we have seen in Chapter 5, to fill out an ancestor research sheet).

Figure 19: Home sources card 1

SAGAR, Samuel James		Family member 8
Home source	Information	Source document number
Family Bible	Father: Benjamin Sagar Mother: Eleanor Marr Photograph of Samuel	1
Letter	Samuel enjoys horse-riding, shooting, cards, races (Flemington Racecourse entry prices mentioned)	2–1
Letter	Wife: Margaret May Seller, b. 6 April 1878	2–2

Figure 20: Home sources card 2

SAGAR, Harry Peter		Family member 4
Home source	Information	Source document number
Family Bible	Father: Samuel James Sagar, b. 27 September 1876	1
Birth certificate	Harry b. 9 March 1899	3–1
Letter	Harry put his age up to join AIF in First World War	2–3

Figure 21: Home sources card 3

SAGAR, Harry Gregory		Family member 2
Home source	Information	Source document number
Marriage certificate	Harry m. Wendy Carol Jones, 28 August 1948	4–1
Diary	Describes hard times growing up in 1930s	5–1
Photograph album	Children's school photographs Family holiday house at Queenscliff	6–1

Next we could continue our exploration of home sources relating to Samuel James Sagar by checking the sources mentioned on the cards of his parents, his wife, his children, his brothers and sisters, and his aunts and uncles. We might, for example, discover, in a letter from his brother to his parents, a mention of Samuel staying with his family while recuperating from an appendix operation. Or we might find, in a letter from an aunt to his mother, caustic comments about a young woman that Samuel seemed to be considering for marriage. (Perhaps this is the only mention of a young woman in his life before his wife and paints a picture of unacceptable behaviour at an entertainment held in a private home!)

From all of this you can see how important your charts, forms, logs and card system are. Organising your findings in this way means you can establish at a relatively early stage what information you have and what you still require. In the case of Samuel James Sagar, we know the basic facts of his life. We know when and where he was born, was married and died. We know his parents' background. And we know where he lived, what his occupation was and what some of his experiences and interests were. Hopefully, by checking through documents, such as letters, we will be able to find out something of his thoughts and feelings, as well. This is important because to create a family history around him we need to know more than just basic or external facts. To make the writing of the history enjoyable, and the finished work interesting for readers, we need to be able to present Samuel as a personality. Many a family history is dull because its leading subject has not been presented as a unique person complete with his or her own approach to life.

Researching the background

To write an interesting history you must understand the times and circumstances in which your ancestors lived. Therefore you need constantly to ask questions about what it was like to grow up at a certain period and in a particular place, what it was like to work in a certain occupation and what opportunities, leisure activities and amenities were available. For example, we could ask the following questions about Samuel James Sagar.

- What did his brothers and sisters do?

- Why did he decide to become a carpenter? Why did he not follow in his father's occupation?

- What educational opportunities were open to him? Did he serve an apprenticeship and, if so, what did this entail?

- Did he work for himself or someone else? Did he have to outlay capital for an apprenticeship or a business?

- What were his conditions of work? For example, what were his hours? Did he enjoy his work?

- What were country towns like when he was growing up? How did his town change over the course of his lifetime?

- What was his standard of living like? What were his various homes like? Did he rent? If he owned a house, did he build it himself? How did his homes compare with those of his parents and children? Did he have more or less time and money for leisure activities than his parents and children? Did those activities vary from theirs?

You will find that answering some of these questions takes you into reading about Australian history. In any case, to write a complete and meaningful history of your family you will need to recreate the general as well as the particular background of your ancestors, because no person lives in a vacuum. National factors such as convict transportation, the gold rushes, pastoral development, land selection, innovations in transport and the growth of cities will probably have had profound effects on the lives of your ancestors. Therefore, in the instance of Samuel James Sagar and his wife Margaret, we might want to ask the following questions.

- Why did their forebears come to Australia? Did economic conditions in the home country (for example, the potato famines if they were Irish) affect their decision, or was there a strong pull from the new country with, for instance, the discovery of gold? Or was the reason for emigration a combination of factors?

- What effect did the 1890s depression have on them?

- What effect did the First World War have on their family?

- What state education was available to them and their children?

- What work opportunities were available to Margaret as a woman? Did women's roles change during her lifetime?

Answering questions such as these will take us to the libraries again.

What records do libraries, genealogical societies and other organisations have?
To fill in the social background of your ancestors check the following sources:

- newspaper articles of the time

- local histories

- general Australian histories of the period

- biographies.

You also need to read family histories written by other people to:

- get a feel for writing one yourself

- find out what makes one family history interesting and another dull

- gain ideas about writing styles, the layout of family histories and the use of photographs, charts and so on.

You will find family histories in libraries and genealogical societies in many forms:

- as published books on the shelves

- as typewritten pamphlets in pamphlet boxes on the shelves

- as typewritten or handwritten pamphlets or series of notes housed in filing cabinets.

Having collected the information you require from libraries, you can next consider visiting local historical society and State museums and collections. Many local museums possess fascinating holdings from earlier periods in Australia. Looking at photographs, newspapers, clothing, machinery and furniture will help you develop a vivid picture of the times you are interested in.

How do I obtain the records I want?
You will already have most relevant records. If not, apply for outstanding certificates and documents, as described in Chapter 4.

Writing the history

Where do I go from here?
You are now ready to write your family history. If you have not previously done much writing, you may be rather hesitant to start. Therefore, begin with the previously mentioned simple exercise of writing about yourself. Proceed as follows:

1. fill out family data and ancestor research sheets for yourself, if you have not already done so

2. draw up a chronological chart for yourself, which records the events and achievements in your life to the present

3. using this chronology as the outline of how your account is to unfold, begin to write

4. make sure that you include in your account experiences you have had and your thoughts and feelings about these, and that you describe the times in which you live, so that future generations as well as present readers will find it interesting and informative

5. ask someone to read your writing and to give you critical comments, then, on the basis of these, write your final version.

Next, complete the same exercise for an ancestor you have chosen as a central character in your family history, by:

1. collecting together all the forms and cards you have for the person, in a ring folder perhaps

2. making a chronological chart of the main dates and events in the ancestor's life, which then forms the basis of your account

3. remembering as you write to incorporate the research you have done on the background and times of the person (see the discussion earlier in the chapter)

4. showing several people your writing for their constructive criticism.

Having completed these preliminary writings, you will feel more confident about executing a detailed history. Keep the following approach in mind as you undertake the task.

- Make a chapter-by-chapter outline of the whole history to ensure that your narrative unfolds logically (this usually means chronologically). Allot chapters according to the importance of the members in your history. For example, a major person may need two chapters, a minor ancestor only one or part of one.

- Plan each chapter in point form, also. Again, this will probably mean establishing a chronology.

- Incorporate the information about historical background that you have obtained from your preparatory research (see the earlier discussion in this chapter).

- Try to restrict yourself to one ancestral line, rather than writing about everyone in each generation. Instead of following all the brothers and sisters of a central person, introduce them only at points where they impinge on his or her life. For example, they may appear in your account of the central ancestor's childhood, schooling, wedding and so on.

Additions to the text

- Charts: read Chapter 1 again and decide which charts you will use. Vertical or horizontal charts are generally used throughout the text and the more elaborate photograph pedigree charts and family trees are incorporated as highlights. Make sure you keep your charts simple and neat and that dates are always included. Remember that the charts you include should contribute to the story.

- Photographs: like charts, they should contribute to the story. Do not just have photographs of one person or one group of people. Try to include photographs that show your reader something about the way people lived at the time. Always place them close to the relevant parts of the text. Remember to give photographs captions and dates where possible.

  One way of using photographs and organising your family history, after you have written up the central ancestor, is to allot facing pages to each of the descendants and his or her spouse. On the left-hand page provide a couple's family data sheet and on the facing page a photograph of them, their names and their pedigree numbers. Under the photograph and caption write a paragraph about what makes the couple special.

- Other illustrations: coats of arms, maps and drawings of family members, houses and so on can enhance the history. Parish maps and maps of the townships and properties where your ancestors lived can be of great interest.

- Bibliography: always include one, annotated if possible, listing all the sources you have used. Use the Further Reading section in this book as a guide. Each entry should contain the author's name, book title, publisher, place of publication and date of publication. Do not make the bibliography too lengthy. An alternative is to number important points throughout the text of each chapter and then provide notes at the end of the chapter.

- Contents page: include a list of the maps, illustrations, photographs and charts used in the book, as well as the chapter titles.

- Index: your family history should include an index to all the names, places and main events mentioned in the text. Because your contents page lists charts and so on, these need not be included in the index. In addition to, or as a substitute for, a conventional index you can use a name index. It provides a clear guide to the people in your family history. Figure 22 gives a sample of entries for such an index.

Figure 22: Name index

Surname	Given names	Born	Married	Died	Occupation and place of	Last known address	Marital state
Davidson	Ella Louise	8 August 1907	7 February 1925	—	Home duties, Ballarat	Smith Street, Ballarat	Married
Sagar	Harry Gregory	27 April 1925	28 August 1948	—	Teacher, Ballarat	Smith Street, Ballarat	Married
Sagar	Jane	13 January 1901	—	6 June 1929	Seamstress, Chiltern	Chiltern	Single

Manuscript preparation

The final manuscript must be able to be easily read, so take some care over its preparation. Consider using one of the following options.

- Use the word processor function of your computer, if you have one. This is easily the most convenient way of preparing a manuscript. Once you have keyed the text in you can change passages, correct spelling and rearrange chapters, headings and so on. With suitable software you can also use your computer to draw charts. (See Chapter 13 for a discussion of computers at greater length.)

- If you do not own a computer and do not yourself type, employ someone to type the manuscript on a word processor or electric typewriter. Check various agencies to get an idea of costs.

Don't forget to take a group photograph at your family reunion.

- If you type the manuscript yourself, use double spacing, allow a wide margin on the left and use a good ribbon so that the typing is clear. Use only one side of a page.

Keep the manuscript pages together in a folder: a ring folder is ideal. (Chapter 7 discusses methods of binding typescript copies and books, if you wish to consider that option once you have made your final changes.)

Once you have completed the final copy of your manuscript, consider holding a family reunion, if you have not already done so. As Chapter 2 has discussed, family reunions are an excellent way of catching up with family members you may not have previously known and of exchanging family stories, information and pedigrees. A family reunion at this time will enable you to double-check the information in your history and to incorporate any further information that comes to hand. You will also be able to review your writing in the light of constructive comments.

7

Publishing your family history

Once you have prepared your manuscript, perhaps held a family reunion and altered the manuscript in the light of further information and comments from family members, you may wish to consider publishing your history. Publishing here means to proceed from the manuscript to multiple copies.

Dom Meadley's book, *Writing a Family History*, is an excellent, readable and clear guide to both writing and publishing a family history, which you should read if you are considering publishing. Another useful book is *How to Write and Publish Your Family History* by Joanna Beaumont. Both books cover publishing in far greater detail than is possible in this chapter.

You will need to decide how you wish to publish your history. There are four alternatives that you can consider.

• Photocopy the typewritten or word processor copy and collate and bind the pages yourself. Bind the copies by stapling along the left-hand side, perhaps covering the staples with strong cloth tape, or by punching holes in the pages and putting each copy in a ring folder, or by using a spiral-binding or Therma-bind machine (see below).

• Send the manuscript to a publisher, but remember that publishers accept only those works considered to have wide public appeal. Generally, you will find that family histories are of interest only to a relatively small market, unless the family members about whom you are writing are particularly prominent citizens.

• Approach a typesetter or printer to organise the typesetting, printing and binding of the book. This is a very expensive way of publishing, so make sure you request a written quotation of costs.

- Publish the book yourself by organising the typesetting and printing. This is cheapest if you opt to publish it in booklet or soft-cover form, rather than in a bound edition.

Should you decide to undertake production or part of it, you will need to complete some or all of the following tasks.

- Discuss type sizes and faces with the typesetter. Prepare the manuscript for typesetting, indicating the size of headings you want and so on. You will need to supply the typesetter with the cover text, title page, contents page, bibliography and index.

- Proofread the typesetter's galleys (photocopies of the typesetting) for mistakes.

- Prepare the pages for the printer to reproduce. This is a very difficult and complex task, so you will need to get advice from your typesetter. For example, print should be of consistent depth and width on all pages (book publishers work on gridded boards) and the printer needs careful instructions about the placement of photographs. You will probably find it easier to have your typesetter prepare the pages for printing.

- Collate the printed pages of each copy and organise the binding yourself. Spiral-binding or Therma-bind machines are available for use at some photocopying centres. The spiral-binding machine punches rectangular holes along the left-hand side of the book and plastic spiral binding is then inserted into these. Covers and binding come in a variety of colours. The Therma-bind machine glues pages together within a soft cover to produce a book resembling a paperback.

Once you have the finished product in your hands, do not forget to give or sell a copy to: family members; your local library; genealogical societies (and include a review copy for their journals); and your State library.

A family history in book form is the result of following step by step the researching, recording and organising of facts recommended in *Tracing Your Family History*. The research is a long and time-consuming task, but the result is well worth the effort. Armed with your knowledge and expertise, you may be tempted to trace further branches of your family and record them on your charts. You may decide to trace another interesting ancestor or to write a history of another branch. Whatever you decide, you have the means to do it. Genealogy quickly becomes a lifelong interest because it involves such exciting detective work: you are always searching for clues, following up new leads, coming to a full stop – and then forging ahead again with renewed enthusiasm.

Part II

Addresses
and
additional
information

8

State and municipal libraries

Addresses

Of the municipal libraries listed below, Kew Library has a particular interest in genealogy, but the others hold many of the works referred to throughout the book and in Further Reading. The abbreviations given in parentheses after the name of the State and municipal libraries are, like those in Table 3, taken from the *National Union Catalogue of Australia* (with the exception of TMRL, VCAU and VKEW) and used widely by libraries.

Australian Capital Territory

National Library of Australia (ANL)
Parkes Place
Canberra 2600

New South Wales

City of Sydney Public
Library (NSPL)
321 Pitt Street
Sydney 2000

Hawkesbury Shire Library (NHKS)
George Street
Windsor 2756

Lake Macquarie City
Library (NLMPL)
Main Road
Speers Point 2284

Mitchell Library (NML)
See State Library of New South Wales

Newcastle Region Public
Library (NNPL)
Local History Department
Laman Street
Newcastle 2300

State Library of New South
Wales (NSL)
General Reference Library
Macquarie Street
Sydney 2000

Willoughby Municipal
Library (NWML)
407 Victoria Avenue
Chatswood 2067

Wollongong City Library (NWPL)
41 Burelli Street
Wollongong East 2520

Northern Territory

Northern Territory Library
Service (XNLS)
Cavenagh Street
Darwin 0801

Queensland

John Oxley Library (QJO)
See State Library of Queensland

State Library of Queensland (QSL)
Queensland Cultural Centre
South Brisbane 4101

South Australia

State Library of South Australia (SSL)
Reference Library
North Terrace
Adelaide 5000

Tasmania

Mersey Regional Library (TMRL)
Oldaker Street
Devonport 7310

State Library of Tasmania (TSL)
91 Murray Street
Hobart 7000

Victoria

Caulfield Library Service (VCAU)
Maple Street
Caulfield 3162

Kew Municipal Library (VKEW)
Civic Centre
Charles Street
Kew 3101

State Library of Victoria (VSL)
304–328 Swanston Street
Melbourne 3000

Western Australia

J. S. Battye Library of Western
Australian History (WJSB)
See State Library Board of Western
Australia

State Library Board of Western
Australia (WLB)
Bibliographical Centre
Alexander Library Building
Perth Cultural Centre
James Street
Perth 6000

9 Government archives and departments

Addresses of archives offices

Some of the works in 'Sources guides', Further Reading, like Nick Vine Hall's *Tracing Your Family History in Australia: A Guide to Sources*, give further details for government archives and departments, such as opening and closing times.

Australian Capital Territory

Australian Archives and Territorial
Archives
Cnr Flemington Road and Stanford
Street
Mitchell 2911
(Director
PO Box 447
Belconnen 2616)

New South Wales

Archives Office of New South Wales
2 Globe Street
Sydney 2000

Australian Archives
Level 1
24 Market Street
Sydney 2000
(Regional Director
PO Box C328
Clarence Street
Sydney 2000)

Northern Territory

Australian Archives
Kelsey Crescent
Nightcliff 0810
(Regional Director
PO Box 293
Darwin 0801)

Queensland

Australian Archives
294 Adelaide Street
Brisbane 4000
(GPO Box 888
Brisbane 4001)

Queensland State Archives
162 Annerley Road
Dutton Park 4102

South Australia

Australian Archives
11–13 Derlanger Avenue
Collinswood 5081
(Regional Director
PO Box 119
Walkerville 5081)

Mortlock Library of South Australiana
State Library of South Australia
North Terrace
Adelaide 5000

Public Record Office of South Australia
Ground Floor
Norwich Centre
55 King William Road
North Adelaide 5006

Tasmania

Archives Office of Tasmania
91 Murray Street
Hobart 7000

Australian Archives
4 Rosny Hill Road
Rosny Park 7018
(GPO Box 1350N
Hobart 7001)

Victoria

Australian Archives
95 Outer Crescent
Middle Brighton 3186
(Regional Director
PO Box 33
Brighton 3186)

Public Record Office of
Victoria (PRO)
City Reference Room
318 Little Bourke Street
Melbourne 3000

PRO
Laverton Base Repository
57 Cherry Lane
Laverton North 3020

PRO
Ballarat Repository
Cnr Mair and Doveton streets
Ballarat 3350

Western Australia

Australian Archives
384 Berwick Street
East Victoria Park 6101
(Regional Director
PO Box 1144
East Victoria Park 6101)

State Archives
Alexander Library Building
Perth Cultural Centre
James Street
Perth 6000

Addresses of supreme courts

Tasmania

Registrar
Supreme Court Registry
Salamanca Place
Hobart 7000

Western Australia

Registrar
Supreme Court of Western Australia
Stirling Gardens
Barrack Street
Perth 6000

Addresses of land titles departments

Australian Capital Territory

Land Titles Office
Allara House
Ground Floor
Cnr Allara Street and
Constitution Avenue
Canberra 2601

New South Wales

Registry of Land Titles and Deeds
Prince Albert Road
Sydney 2000

Northern Territory

Department of Law
Land Titles
Nichols Place
Cnr Cavenagh and Bennett streets
Darwin 0800
(GPO Box 3021
Darwin 0801)

Queensland

Department of Mapping and Surveying
Sunmap Centre
State Government Building
Anzac Square
Adelaide Street
Brisbane 4000

Lands Department
Land Administration Building
George Street
Brisbane 4000

Titles Office
State Government Building
Anzac Square
Brisbane 4000

South Australia

General Registry Office
Registrar-General's Office
Department of Lands
Colonel Light Centre
25 Pirie Street
Adelaide 5000

Land Tenure Administration
Department of Lands
Wakefield House
Cnr Wakefield Street
and Gawler Place
Adelaide 5000

Lands Titles Office
Department of Lands
Colonel Light Centre
25 Pirie Street
Adelaide 5000

Tasmania

Land Titles and Deeds Office
15 Murray Street
Hobart 7000

Victoria

Department of Conservation,
Forests and Lands
240–250 Victoria Parade
East Melbourne 3002

Registrar of Titles
Title Office
283 Queen Street
Melbourne 3000

Registrar-General's Office
Law Department
5th Floor
233 William Street
Melbourne 3000

Western Australia

Office of Titles
Law Chambers
Cathedral Square
Perth 6000

Addresses of probate offices

Australian Capital Territory

Registrar of Probates
Law Courts of Australian Capital Territory
1st Floor
Knowles Place
Canberra 2601

New South Wales

Probate Division
Supreme Court of New South Wales
5th Floor
Law Courts Building
Queens Square
Sydney 2000

Northern Territory

Registrar of Probates
Probate Registry
Supreme Court of Northern Territory
Law Courts Building
Mitchell Street
Darwin 0800

South Australia

Probate Registry
Supreme Court of South Australia
301 King William Street
Adelaide 5000

Tasmania

Probate Registry
Supreme Court of Tasmania
Salamanca Place
Hobart 7000

Victoria

Registrar of Probates
Probate and Administration
Office
Law Courts
Nubrik House
271 William Street
Melbourne 3000

Western Australia

Probate Office
Stirling Gardens
Barrack Street
Perth 6000

Public Trust Office
7th Floor
565 Hay Street
Perth 6000

10

Genealogical societies

General genealogical societies: addresses, interests and services

Australian Capital Territory

Heraldry and Genealogy Society of Canberra

Iluka Street
Narrabundah 2604
(GPO Box 585
Canberra 2601)

Classes
In July each year the Society conducts a basic course on the techniques and sources of family history research. Course notes are published at regular intervals (see below).

Library
This contains reference books, members' interests registers, journals from other Australian and overseas genealogical societies, microfilm and microfiche records and cemetery records. Open Days are held at the library to inform the public of resources available for family history research.

Journal
The Society's quarterly journal, *Ancestral Searcher*, contains: genealogical news; 'Hot Sources' (information regarding location of little-known resource material); readers' enquiries; computer news; book reviews; and news from interstate and overseas genealogical societies.

Other publications

One of its major publications is *Family History for Beginners*, which contains the course notes from the beginners' course and is regularly updated.

New South Wales

Society of Australian Genealogists (SAG)

Richmond Villa
120 Kent Street
Sydney 2000

Classes

In 1974 SAG instituted the Diploma of Family Historical Studies (Dip. FHS) course to accredit genealogists. It is open to all.

Special interest group

There is a Computer Users Group for all those interested in genealogical computing (see Chapter 13).

Library

This is the largest non-governmental genealogical reference library in Australia. It contains:

- over 10 000 volumes in its Australian and Overseas Collection, including many bound sets of periodicals and journals and many reference books relating to overseas countries

- Australian family histories, local histories and genealogical reference books

- more than 600 000 cards in its General Index Collection, which is continually added to by members and contains reference material relating mainly to people who have resided in Australia, particularly in New South Wales

- manuscript collections containing many genealogies compiled by members, research notes, diaries, business records, family papers, newspaper clippings and similar documents

- microfilm collection of Australian and overseas records, which gives information on millions of names. For many years the Society has been microfilming original church registers, many of which have never been copied before. These are held at the Society's Annexe, 8 Argyle Street, Sydney 2000.

Journal

The Society's quarterly magazine, *Descent*, contains: genealogical articles; book reviews; notes and news of forthcoming genealogical events in Australia and overseas; notices concerning family reunions and a members' research enquiry section; information about their publications for sale; and a computer column.

Other publications

The Society has published *Guide to the Library 1984*, which covers the holdings of its library, Nancy Gray's *Compiling Your Family History* and *Roots and Branches: Ancestry for Australians* by E. J. Lea-Scarlett.

Northern Territory

Genealogical Society of the Northern Territory

PO Box 37212
Winnellie 5789

Library

2nd Floor
State Reference Library
Darwin 5790

The library contains research aids, such as indexes of births, deaths and marriages for all Australian States, post office directories, shipping records, research directories, maps, gazettes, armed services information, cemetery indexes and international research publications, for example the *St Catherine's House Index*.

Classes

Courses on family history research techniques are conducted from time to time.

Journal

The Society's quarterly magazine, *Progenitor*, includes: articles and news of the Society; readers' enquiries; and book reviews.

Other publications

Records on microfiche include: *Censuses* 1881, 1891 and 1901; *Lone Graves of the Northern Territory 1839–1976*; the *Index of the Northern Territory Justices of the Peace, Special Magistrates, Barristers and Solicitors, Practitioners and Notaries 1839–1965*; the *Alien's Index*, giving births 1888–1922 and deaths 1875–1922; *Overlanders (or Drovers) Arriving in the Northern Territory 1879–1883*; *Mining Permits 1896–1911*; indexes to various mortuary records and cemetery transcriptions.

Further microfiche to be produced will include: schedule of land transactions; pastoral leases; pastoral permits; applications for mineral land; gold-mining leases; colonial applications for land; applications for extended land; and some shipping information.

Queensland

Genealogical Society of Queensland (GSQ)

> PO Box 423
> Woolloongabba 4102

The Society has branches throughout the State.

Special interest groups

These meet on a bi-monthly basis and have been formed to assist members and the exchange of information in specialised areas. They include:

- Scottish Group
- Irish Group
- German Group
- Scandinavian Group
- Computer Users Group.

Library

> Woolloongabba Post Office
> Woolloongabba 4102

The Society's Resource Centre contains cemetery records collected from all over Australia and overseas, microfiche and microfilm records, including the *International Genealogical Index*, all Registrar-General's records released to date for each State of Australia, probate indexes, Queensland post office directories and New South Wales shipping records and convict records. It also has a vast collection of printed records, a large collection of family histories, local and school histories and publications from other genealogical societies in Australia.

Classes

Educational classes on genealogy, covering the basics of genealogy as well as advanced genealogical research, are conducted on a regular basis at the Resource Centre.

Journals

The Society's journal, *Generation*, is published quarterly. Newsletters are issued occasionally.

Queensland Family History Society (QFHS)

> PO Box 171
> Indooroopilly 4068

Special interest groups

These include:

- Central European Group
- Devon–Cornwall Group
- Lancashire Group
- Computer Group.

The Society's Adoption Scheme for Remote Area Members (ASRAM) links country members with city members; the city members undertake research for the country members when the latter are unable to do it themselves.

Library

> Upstairs
> Cnr Campbell and
> Tufton streets
> Bowen Hills 4006

The library contains a substantial collection of reference books and overseas journals, the *International Genealogical Index*, an ever-growing index of cemetery and monumental inscriptions and the *St Catherine's House Index*. It also has a library loan scheme for country members. It offers a limited printout service for microfiche.

Journal

The bi-monthly journal of the Society, *Queensland Family Historian*, contains: genealogical articles; 'Help Wanted' queries for members; members' interests register; society news; and information regarding education workshops.

Other publications

These include: *Letters from Emigrants to Queensland 1863–1885*; J. O'Sullivan's *A Short Guide to Tracing Your Convict Ancestry*; *Strays Collection Australasia* compiled by Rae Hopkinson; *Name Directory of Moreton Bay Region* for 1850–1851, 1852–1853 and 1854–1855, compiled by M. Eastgate; and *Open Day Papers* which consists of *Queensland Research Guide* (1982), *Man on the Land* (1985), *A Grave Look at Family History* (1986) and *Our Migratory Ancestors* (1987).

As a Bicentenary project the Society is indexing Queensland primary resources for the period up to 1860. In 1988 an index will be produced of all people who were resident in Queensland during this early period.

South Australia

South Australian Genealogy and Heraldry Society

> 201 Unley Road
> Unley 5061
> (GPO Box 592
> Adelaide 5001)

Library

The library contains extensive resources, such as cemetery records, archival material and published works.

Journal

The *South Australian Genealogist* is published four times a year. It contains: book reviews; general articles on family history; readers' enquiries; and Society news.

Other publications

The Society has published the *Biographical Index of South Australians 1836–1885*, compiled by Jill Statton.

Tasmania

Genealogical Society of Tasmania

19 Cambridge Road
Bellerive 7018
(GPO Box 640G
Hobart 7001)

Library

The library contains useful resources and published works.

Journal

Tasmanian Ancestry comes out four times a year. It contains: genealogical articles; Society news; and book reviews.

Victoria

Genealogical Society of Victoria

5th Floor
Curtin House
252 Swanston Street
Melbourne 3000

Special interest groups

- Port Phillip Pioneers Group: members are those who can prove descent from an early settler in the Port Phillip District of the Colony of New South Wales before 1 July 1851, when it became the separate Colony of Victoria.

- 1850s Group: membership open to those who can prove direct descent from a settler who arrived and settled in the Colony of Victoria between 1 July 1851 and 31 December 1859, that is, the early gold rush years.

- Descendants of Convicts Group: membership open only to those who can prove direct descent from a convict transported to Australia.

- International Settlers Group: membership open to those with international ancestry, that is, those from countries other than the British Isles.

- Victorian Genealogists Using Microcomputers (GUM): see Chapter 13.

- Country groups: apply to the Society for groups in different country areas.

Library

This is a reference library, so its contents cannot be borrowed. Photocopying is available, as well as equipment for viewing microfiche and microfilm. Holdings include a catalogued collection of books, manuscripts, microfilms, family histories, local histories, cemetery records, indexes to births, deaths and marriages, parish registers and periodicals of kindred societies and on related subjects. It is open to the public for a fee.

Journal

The Society's quarterly journal, *Ancestor*, contains: genealogical information; details of the activities of the Society and its special interest groups; a section on members' queries, which enables members to exchange details of ancestry; and lists of new books and records.

Other publications

Directory of Members' Interests, 1981–1982, 1983–1984 and 1987–1988 (on microfiche also), is compiled from questionnaires sent out to members. Its aim is to link people searching for information about the same families. It contains 20 000 entries and is available for purchase.

Australian Institute of Genealogical Studies

PO Box 68
Oakleigh 3166

Library

1st Floor
Uniting Church Hall
Cnr Eddy Street and Halley Avenue
Hartwell 3124

This is a reference library whose holdings include books, periodicals, parish registers, directories, indexes to births, deaths and marriages, microfilm and microfiche records and so on. Regular working bees and library assistants' training courses are held.

Journal

The Institute's quarterly journal, the *Genealogist*, contains: genealogical articles; news of the Institute; articles on records and sources; and new accessions to the library.

Western Australia

Genealogical Society of Western Australia

Library

> 5/48 May Street
> Bayswater 6053

This is a reference library containing genealogical publications, journals of other societies, a collection of family histories and so on.

Journal

The *Western Ancestor*, published four times a year, contains: readers' enquiries; genealogical articles and news; and book reviews.

Special interest groups

Meetings are held at the library (dates on application). Present groups are:

- Descendants of Colonial Convicts
- Irish Group
- Scottish Group
- South Australian Group
- Computer Interest Group
- Victorian Group
- European Group.

Other publications

The Society has produced or is in the process of producing: directories of members' interests; a library catalogue; microfiche of transcriptions of cemetery inscriptions in Western Australia; lists of overseas passenger arrivals at the port of Albany 1873–1925; and indexes of deaths based on *West Australian* notices 1907–1920.

Church of Jesus Christ of Latter-day Saints Genealogical Department: addresses, holdings and services

Because of its emphasis on family relationships, both present and past, the Church of Jesus Christ of Latter-day Saints is committed to genealogical research and the preservation of records. The Church's Genealogical Department in the United States of America has microfilmed millions of records from many countries to assist its members in genealogical research and as a worldwide service to the preservation of records. These microfilms are copies of birth, death, marriage and other records and are collectively known as the *International Genealogical Index* (IGI).

The original IGI microfilms are stored in underground vaults near Salt Lake City. They are indexed a few kilometres from the vaults, in the main genealogical library of the Church at Salt Lake City. Copies of records are made available to the public at no charge through the hundreds of branch libraries around the world. Inter-library loan arrangements by these branch libraries ensure that the records are available to anyone engaged in genealogical research.

Voluntary library assistants will help you as much as they are able. Microfiche readers are available at most branches. As well as the IGI, branch libraries hold records such as: parish registers; gazetteers; census records; civil registration records; family histories; histories; military records; probates, deeds and so on. However, each library differs from the others in its immediate holdings.

The following list of libraries of the Latter-day Saints Genealogical Department is mainly concerned with branches in the capital city of each State. Check with these for locations of additional libraries in country areas.

Australian Capital Territory

Cnr Wattle and Brigalow streets
Lyneham 2602

New South Wales

5 Nalya Close
Charlestown 2290

55 Greenwich Road
Greenwich 2065

Pringle Road
Hebersham 2770

74 Walter Street
Mortdale 2223

169 Pennant Street
Parramatta 2150

Northern Territory

Cnr Trower and Sabine roads
Milner 0810

Queensland

Eight Mile Plains Chapel
Underwood Road
Eight Mile Plains
Brisbane 4123

200 River Terrace
Kangaroo Point
Brisbane 4169

St Paul's Place
Isle of Capri 4217

Fulham Road
Gulliver
Townsville 4812

South Australia

Cutting Road
Marion 5043

Von Braun Crescent
Modbury North 5092

Dunn Street
Port Pirie 5540

99 Jenkins Avenue
Whyalla 5600

Tasmania

15 Elmsleigh Road
Glenorchy 7010

Victoria

285 Heidelberg Road
Northcote 3070

Cnr Cathies Lane and Pumps Road
Wantirna 3152

Western Australia

308 Preston Point Road
Attadale 6156

163 Wordsworth Avenue
Yokine 6060

11

Registries of births, deaths and marriages

Holdings and addresses

Australian Capital Territory

Registrar of Births, Deaths and Marriages
Allara House
Allara Street
Canberra 2601
(PO Box 788
Canberra 2601)

Registration of births, deaths and marriages commenced in the Australian Capital Territory on 1 January 1930. Registration is confined to events occurring within the Territory. Events which occurred prior to this date are registered in New South Wales and therefore must be applied for there.

New South Wales

Principal Register of Births, Deaths and Marriages
50 Bridge Street
Sydney 2001
(GPO Box 30
Sydney 2001)

Northern Territory

Registrar Births, Deaths and Marriages
Nichols Place
Cnr Cavenagh and Bennett streets
Darwin 0801
(GPO Box 3021
Darwin 0801)

For Alice Springs district:

Deputy Registrar
PO Box 8043
Alice Springs 0871

Registration of births, deaths and marriages commenced in the Northern Territory in 1870.

Queensland

Registrar-General's Office
Old Treasury Building
Brisbane 4000
(PO Box 188
Brisbane North Quay 4002)

Registration of births, deaths and marriages commenced in Queensland in 1855. The church records kept prior to that date are incomplete.

South Australia

Principal Registrar
Births, Deaths and Marriages Registration Division
Department of Public and Consumer Affairs, South Australia
Edmund Wright House
59 King William Street
Adelaide 5000
(GPO Box 1351
Adelaide 5001)

Registration of births, deaths and marriages commenced in South Australia from 1 July 1842 and indexes to events are available to 1906.

Tasmania

Registrar-General
15 Murray Street
Hobart 7000
(GPO Box 541F
Hobart 7001)

Records held by this Registry date from 1900. Records prior to 1900 are under the control of the Archives Office of Tasmania. Records of baptism, marriage and burial contained in church registers for the period 1803–1838 have been incorporated into records held at the Archives Office and are available for search. Statutory records of births, deaths and marriages were made from 1839 in various district registers and transcripts of these are also available. However, information furnished by early records is scanty in comparison with that of more recent ones. Enquiries about registrations before 1900 should be directed to:

Principal Archivist
Archives Office of Tasmania
91 Murray Street
Hobart 7000

Victoria

Registry of Births, Deaths and Marriages
295 Queen Street
Melbourne 3000
(GPO Box 4332
Melbourne 3000)

Western Australia

Registrar-General's Office
Oakleigh Building
22 St George's Terrace
Perth 6000

Compulsory registration of births, deaths and marriages commenced in Western Australia during the latter half of 1841. The Office has copies of all the registrations since that time. Prior to 1896 the registrations contain rather limited information.

Microfiche of the *Index of Births, Deaths and Marriages 1841–1905* can be viewed at the Library Board of Western Australia. Certain church records relating to baptisms, burials and marriages prior to 1841 are also held there. Enquiries should be directed to:

Library Board of Western Australia
Alexander Library Building
Perth Cultural Centre
Perth 6000

Charges

The following charges are provided to give you an idea of the cost involved in obtaining certificates of births, deaths and marriages. The fees given are current for May 1988, but may increase.

Australian Capital Territory

Charges are for certificates of births, deaths and marriages after 1 January 1930 within the Territory.

Copy of full certificate, including search (unlimited number of years)	$12.00
Copy of extract	$ 8.00
Priority fee (in addition to normal fee)	$10.00

New South Wales

Copy of full certificate, including search of a five-year span	$14.00
Copy of certificate where registration number quoted	$10.00
Search fee for additional ten-year span	$ 5.00
Priority fee	$ 9.00

The holdings of historical museums will help you to visualise the past, if you are writing the history of your family or an ancestor.

Northern Territory

Payment is payable to Receiver of Territory Monies.

Copy of full certificate, including search of a five-year span	$ 8.00
Copy of extract (name, date and place)	$ 8.00
Copy of long extract (name date, place and parents)	$ 8.00

Queensland

Copy of full certificate, including search of a five-year span	$14.50
Copy of extract	$ 8.50
Search fee for additional five-year span	$ 7.50
Priority fee	$ 7.50

South Australia

Copy of certificate, including search of a five-year span	$13.00
Copy of extract	$13.00
Search fee for additional five-year span	$13.00
Priority fee	$11.00

Tasmania

Note that you do not need to send payment to the Archives Office until it advises you of the charges incurred.

Copy of full certificate, including search of a five-year span	$12.00
Copy of extract	$ 8.00
Search fee for additional five-year span	$ 6.00

Victoria

For early church records 1837–1853 and civil records from 1853 on.

Copy of full certificate, including search of a five-year span	$22.00
Copy of certificate where registration number quoted	$11.00
Copy of extract	$11.00
Search fee for additional five-year span	$11.00
Priority fee	$20.00

Western Australia

Copy of full certificate, including five-year search	$15.00
Copy of extract (name, date and place of event and including search of a five-year span)	$10.00
Search fee for additional five-year span	$ 5.00
Priority fee	$10.00

12

Professional researchers

Addresses

Some organisations, such as genealogical societies, will on request supply a list of professional searchers who are familiar with the holdings of that particular organisation. Lists of researchers may also be found in some State libraries and in the Telecom *Yellow Pages* directory.

The Australasian Association of Genealogists and Record Agents (AAGRA) offers the public the services of reliable and competent professional genealogists and search agents, because its membership is only open to well-qualified people with considerable practical experience in the field. Integrity and confidentiality concerning the client's affairs are required of members. Requests should be addressed to:

> Secretary
> AAGRA
> PO Box 268
> Oakleigh 3166

Fees are a private matter between the person requiring information and the professional researcher.

13

Note on using computers in genealogy

Uses in genealogy

Computers can be used to good advantage in genealogy. As you progress in your research you amass an enormous amount of information, which needs to be organised. This may be done by the methods outlined in Chapters 1–5, but using computers is an alternative that should not be overlooked, particularly if you already possess a home computer or have the means and need to buy one.

What is a computer?

A computer is an electronic device that performs calculations and processes information. It can handle vast numbers of facts and figures and solve complicated problems at high speeds.

The hardware, that is, the machinery, that makes up a computer system consists of: the central processing unit; an electronic keyboard for entering information; a visual display unit or monitor; and a printer. Information is often stored on floppy disks, in which case a disk drive becomes an essential part of the hardware.

The computer needs to be programmed to process information in particular ways. So in addition to hardware you will require software, that is, a computer program. There are many computer programs available for purchase. A word-processing package, for example, could also be used for letter writing. When information is processed, a printed copy is often needed so a system that includes a printer becomes necessary. When selecting your system make sure that it has the capacity to do all that you require of it.

Why use a computer?

- It is an excellent means of recording and storing your data.

- It provides an efficient method of organising your data and indexing it for easy retrieval.

- In general it saves time and effort.

- With suitable software, it can be used to draw up your charts and forms in a clear and legible manner.

- Its word processor function enables you to write letters and record correspondence, and to write your family history.

Choosing a computer for genealogy

Your choice of a computer will generally depend on your needs and requirements, which will, of course, be dictated by your present genealogical interests. Generally the greater the computer capacity the greater the cost.

The particular needs and requirements of a computer for genealogy are:

- an ability to store and process an enormous amount of data – the computer you choose will depend on the capacity for storage you require and how easily it retrieves data

- an extensive memory because in genealogy there is a lot of indexing and sorting of data

- a printer to print your data

- a word-processing component for writing letters and possibly your family history

- a simple data base, or filing system, for names, addresses, dates, correspondence and so on

- compatibility with other computers and accessibility, in case you want to change over to a more powerful system at a later date or exchange information with others in the field by means of a telephone link or disks.

To decide which computer and what software you need you should:

- read computer articles and magazines (see 'Computers in genealogy', Further Reading)

- read books on the subject, especially those written for genealogists (see 'Computers in genealogy', Further Reading)

- join a computer group for genealogists in your State.

The following list of genealogical groups with a special interest in computers will help you get in contact and join. If the list does not give a users group for your State, contact your local genealogical society.

Genealogical society groups using computers

New South Wales

Society of Australian Genealogists Computer Users Group

> SAG Computer Users Group
> Richmond Villa
> 120 Kent Street
> Sydney 2000

This group meets once a month and offers a venue for enthusiasts wishing to exchange information and share their interest in genealogical computing. Topics discussed include selection of a computer, problem solving and whatever is of interest to members. Computer news from the Group is contained in the 'Computer Column' of SAG's journal, *Descent*.

The Group has been involved in a project for several years to implement the *Australasian Genealogical Computer Index* (AGCI). The aim of the project is to provide family historians with a quick, easy-to-use method of locating genealogical information within the SAG library and other record centres in Australia and New Zealand.

Queensland

Queensland Family History Society Computer Group

> QFHS Computer Group
> PO Box 171
> Indooroopilly 4068

The Group is for members interested in what can be done with computers in the field of genealogy and for members who have computers or intend to buy one. Meetings are held bi-monthly.

South Australia

South Australian Computer Interest Group

South Australian Computer Interest Group
C/o South Australian Genealogy and Heraldry Society
201 Unley Road
Unley 5061
(GPO Box 592
Adelaide 5001)

The Group is part of the South Australian Genealogy and Heraldry Society and meets monthly. Its aim is to help those who already have computers and genealogical software. It also encourages other members to use computers as an aid to their family history research.

Victoria

Genealogists Using Microcomputers

GUM
Genealogical Society of Victoria
5th Floor
252 Swanston Street
Melbourne 3000

This is a special interest group of the Genealogical Society of Victoria, which provides for the exchange and sharing of computer information among members of all levels of experience in both computers and genealogy. It publishes a newsletter, *Victorian GUM*, organises talks and provides a checklist and advice for members buying computers.

14 Bookshops

Addresses and special interests

Here is a list of some bookshops that specialise in genealogy and family, local and general history. Note also that many genealogical societies have their own bookshops.

New South Wales

Bountiful Books
Burnside Village
Blackwood Place
North Parramatta 2151

This is a specialist genealogy bookstore carrying titles on most aspects of family history research, as well as a complete range of related wall charts, posters and stationery forms.

Family Tree Shop
Old Sydney Town
Gosford 2250
(PO Box 38
Gosford 2250)

Australia's Heritage Bookshop
81½ George Street
The Rocks
Sydney 2000
(Library of Australian History
PO Box 795
North Sydney 2060)

The Bookshop specialises in reference and research publications, local and regional histories for all Australian States, university press titles and family history and genealogical publications, and it provides an annotated catalogue of publications in print through its mail order service.

South Australia

Gould Books
Retreat Valley Road
Gumeracha 5233
(PO Box 126
Gumeracha 5233)

The shop offers a very comprehensive range of books in the areas of genealogy and family, local and Australian history, and it also has maps and charts. On request (and for payment) it will provide an annotated catalogue of publications.

Victoria

D. J. and A. D. Browning Booksellers
PO Box 1001
Ringwood 3134

The firm specialises in English and Welsh family and local history books. Send a stamped, self-addressed envelope to the above address to receive a book catalogue.

Family Heritage Services
10 Harding Street
Winchelsea 3241

The service supplies books and stationery and undertakes research. Its aim is to provide a complete genealogical service to family historians.

McBeth Genealogical Books
PO Box 136
Hampton 3188

This is not a bookshop, but Ms McBeth provides a mail order service for books and does research.

Further reading

Indexes to births, deaths and marriages

The following indexes to births, deaths and marriages are the ones currently available. They are all on microfiche.

Australia

Young, Faye, and Harris, Don. *Birth, Death and Marriage Certificates in Australia.* Australian Institute of Genealogical Studies, Oakleigh, 1984.
   Booklet with tables showing what information is given on birth, death and marriage certificates in all States and the Australian Capital Territory and Northern Territory for any period. It also includes addresses, fees and notes on public access and indexes, but these are no longer completely up to date.

Australian Capital Territory

Pre-1930 see New South Wales, Registry of Births, Deaths and Marriages entries.

New South Wales

New South Wales, Registry of Births, Deaths and Marriages. *Indexes to Births, Deaths and Marriages 1788–1899.*
New South Wales, Registry of Births, Deaths and Marriages. *Indexes to Births, Deaths and Marriages 1900–1905.*

Northern Territory

Pre-1870 see South Australia, Registry of Births, Deaths and Marriages entry.

Queensland

Queensland, Registry of Births, Deaths and Marriages. *Indexes to Baptisms, Deaths and Marriages 1856–1899.* (Births 1850–1869 only.)

South Australia

South Australia, Registry of Births, Deaths and Marriages. *Indexes to Births, Deaths and Marriages 1842–1906.*

Tasmania

Archives Office of Tasmania. *Indexes and Registers of Births, Deaths and Marriages 1803–1899.*

Tasmania, Registry of Births, Deaths and Marriages. *Indexes of Births, Deaths and Marriages Post 1900.*

Victoria

Historical Records of Victoria, vol. 3. Victorian Government Printing Office, Melbourne, 1981–1984.
    See ch. 38, 'Marriages, Births and Deaths, 1836–1839', for contents of clergymen's registers from their commencement to 1839.

Victoria, Registry of Births, Deaths and Marriages. *Index to Births 1/1/1837–31/12/1895.*

Victoria, Registry of Births, Deaths and Marriages. *Index to Deaths 1/7/1837–31/12/1913.*

Victoria, Registry of Births, Deaths and Marriages. *Index to Early Church Records 1/1/1837–30/6/1853.*

Victoria, Registry of Births, Deaths and Marriages. *Index to Marriages 1/7/1837–31/12/1913.*

Western Australia

Perth, Registrar-General's Office. *Indexes to Births, Deaths and Marriages 1841–1905.*

General directories and indexes

The post office directories included here give information about householders' names, trades and professions and inhabitants of a particular area by street, suburb or town. Different libraries will have these in microfiche and/or book form.

New South Wales

Archives Authority of New South Wales. *Genealogical Research Kit.* 1986.
    Documents the arrival of convicts, assisted immigrants and unassisted people in New South Wales, 1788–1900, as well as records of births, deaths and marriages, naturalisation, employment of public servants, land grants, publicans' licences, electoral rolls and so on. Four stages in all are planned for this Bicentennial Project; Stages 1 and 2 are now available.

Genealogical Society of Victoria. *Index to the New South Wales Convict Indents 1780–1842.*

It gives an introduction and then an alphabetical list of ships and names of convicts arranged alphabetically by surname.

Mouritz, J. J. *Port Phillip Directory 1847–   .*

Lists over 5000 residents of the Port Phillip District of New South Wales before the gold rushes.

Sydney Directory 1851–   . Comp. W. Ford and F. Ford.

Gives the streets of Sydney arranged alphabetically and lists the residents of each. More than 5000 citizens are mentioned.

Queensland

Wise's Post Office Directory 1896–1949.

South Australia

Sands and McDougall's Post Office Directory 1887–1958.
Wise's Post Office Directory 1897–1908.

Tasmania

Walch's Tasmanian Almanac 1863–1934.
Wise's Post Office Directory 1894–1948.

Victoria

Baillière, F. *Official Post Office Directory of Victoria 1868–1881.*
Baillière's Victorian Gazetteers, 1865, 1870, 1879.

It is an invaluable tool for your research because it gives information on towns, rivers, creeks, mountains, goldfields, roads, railways and squatters' stations in Victoria at particular times. It provides descriptions of places and a number of details. For example, the name of a station may be accompanied by the owner's name and mention of a town will include details of population and industry.

Butler and Brooke's National Directory of Victoria 1868–1881.
Port Phillip/Victoria Directories 1839–1900.
Sands and McDougall's Melbourne Directories 1862–1911.
Sands and McDougall's Victorian Directories 1912–1974.
Wise's Victoria Post Office Directory 1884–1900 (1886–1887, 1890 not covered).

Research directories

All genealogical societies keep directories of members' interests in one form or another.

Genealogical Research Directory: National and International, 1987: And Guide to Genealogical Societies. Eds Keith A. Johnson, and Malcolm R. Sainty. Library of Australian History, North Sydney, 1987.

Very convenient and useful annual national and international instrument for exchange of research information. It welcomes entries from interested people and contains a list of main events, such as conferences, in genealogy world-wide and a directory of societies.

Genealogical Society of Victoria. *Directory of Members' Interests.* Genealogical Society of Victoria, Melbourne, 1981.

Compiled from questionnaires sent out to Society members, its aim is to link people searching for information about the same families.

Sources guides

These provide guides to the locations of sources and their hours and addresses.

Australia

Ansell, L. J. *Register of Church Archives: A Select Guide to Resource Material in Australia.* Church Archivists' Society, Toowoomba, 1985.

Important guide to church archives.

Hansen, Neil. *Guide to Genealogical Sources in Australia and New Zealand.* Halls, Melbourne, 1962.

A good basic guide, soundly researched, but does need to be used with more recent guides in order to get more up-to-date details of, for example, fees, opening times and addresses.

Lay, Patricia. *A Guide to Genealogical and Family History Resources in the National Library of Australia.* Patricia Lay, Queanbeyan, 1986.

A comprehensive guide to genealogical and family history resources in the National Library of Australia, aimed at helping you to locate independently items relevant to your interest.

Roll Call: A Guide to Genealogical Sources in the Australian War Memorial. Australian War Memorial, Canberra, 1986.

A comprehensive guide to the Australian armed forces sources held in the Australian War Memorial.

Vine Hall, Nick. *Tracing Your Family History in Australia: A Guide to Sources.* Rigby, Adelaide, 1985.

A good State-by-State coverage of sources and historical background, the best coverage being given to New South Wales.

New South Wales

Society of Australian Genealogists. *Guide to the Library 1984.* Society of Australian Genealogists, Sydney, 1984.

It covers the holdings of the Society's library.

Queensland

McIntyre, Perry. *The Queensland Source Book: A Guide to the Repositories and Resources Available to the Local Historian in Queensland, Australia.* Blackwater, Brisbane, 1986.

Covers areas such as genealogical and historical societies, sources of the Church of Jesus Christ of Latter-day Saints, Australian and State archives, John Oxley Library, indexes to births, deaths and marriages, maps, land records and the National Trust. It includes useful addresses and books.

South Australia

Peake, Andrew. *Sources for South Australian History*. South Australian Genealogy and Heraldry Society, Adelaide, 1987.
Covers major sources available in South Australia.

Ragless, Margaret E. *Yesterday for Tomorrow: A Guide to South Australian Historical Research*. Margaret E. Ragless, Hawthorndene, 1982.
Introduction to sources for South Australian research. Provides an annotated list of selected records, including directories, parliamentary papers, government and Education Department gazettes and so on.

Victoria

Brown, Frances. *Notes on Victorian Family History*. Library Council of Victoria, Melbourne, 1987.
Very useful set of notes giving a summary of the resources held in both the La Trobe Collection and the Main Reference Library of the State Library of Victoria.

Brown, Frances, Meadley, Dom, and Morgan, Marjorie (eds). *Family and Local History Sources in Victoria*. Custodians of Records, Blackburn, 1985.
An absolute 'must' for Victorians, as it lists locations of sources Victoria-wide, with their opening times, addresses and holdings. Very comprehensive and easy to follow.

Genealogical Sources. Public Record Office, Melbourne, 1985.
Pamphlet outlining the holdings of the Victorian Public Record Office and how to use them, and giving information about registration certificates and so on.

Guides to genealogy

Bridging the Generations: Fourth Australasian Congress on Genealogy and Heraldry, Canberra, 1986. Comp. Geoffrey Burkhardt, and Peter Proctor. Heraldry and Genealogy Society of Canberra, Canberra, 1986.
Highly recommended. Gives proceedings of the Congress and the bulk of the papers delivered, covering all aspects of genealogy and the latest developments.

Family History for Beginners. Heraldry and Genealogy Society of Canberra, Canberra, 1985.
A concise, how-to-do-it book written as a result of a series of beginners' courses run by the Society.

Gobble, J. R. *What to Say in Your Genealogical Letters*. Gobble, Idaho, 1980.
A practical dos and don'ts approach to writing genealogical correspondence.

Gray, Nancy. *Compiling Your Family History: A Guide to Procedure*. Society of Australian Genealogists, Sydney, 1985.
Gives a very good outline of research procedure.

McLachlan, Eve. *Interviewing Elderly Relatives*. Federation of Family History Societies, London, 1985.
Book on collecting family information, recording it, sticky starts, questioning techniques, family traditions and finding unknown relatives.

Linder, Bill R. *How to Trace Your Family History*. Everest House, New York, 1978.

Basic guide to tracing your ancestors, with an excellent section on hints for writing good letters.

Puttock, A. G. *Tracing Your Family Tree for Australians and New Zealanders.* Lothian, Melbourne, 1981.

Good guide to tracing your family tree, which describes three different pedigree charts, giving the advantages and disadvantages of each.

Reakes, Janet. *The A–Z Genealogical Handbook.* Methuen, North Ryde, 1986.

In alphabetical form it covers clearly and concisely all the different aspects of researching your family and includes useful sections on how to save money, date discrepancies, adoption, computers and so on.

_____. *A Guide to Tracing Missing Ancestors.* Genealogy Research Service Centre, Bass Hill, 1986.

Good book to refer to if you have any problems or stumbling blocks in your research.

Rogers, Colin. *The Family Tree Detective: A Manual for Anyone Who Has English or Welsh Ancestors, to Help Them Analyse and Solve Genealogical Problems, 1538 to the Present Day.* Collins, Sydney, 1985.

Emphasises alternative steps to take when your research meets a 'dead end' and advises you about sources and basic methods in Britain.

Squires, Debra, and Barraclough, Linda. *Planning a Family Reunion.* Kapana Press, Bairnsdale, 1983.

Offers practical advice on all aspects of reunions, including gathering the family, your family history, planning the programme, displays, ideas, recording the day and so on.

State Library of Victoria. Genealogy Procedures Manual. Unpublished.

A looseleaf manual in three folders, which gives clear guidelines on the use of a variety of sources, such as directories and electoral rolls. Folder 1 gives information on the use of indexes to births, marriages and deaths; folder 2 gives notes on electoral rolls, the use of directories like Sands and McDougall's and so on; folder 3 gives a guide to convict records and an index to naturalisation and includes a list of professional researchers.

Biographical dictionaries

Australian Dictionary of Biography 1788–1939, 10 vols. Melbourne University Press, Melbourne, 1966–1986.

Invaluable source of information on people in Australian history.

Biographical Index of South Australians 1836–1885, 4 vols. Ed. Jill Statton. South Australian Genealogy and Heraldry Society, Marden, 1986.

Contains biographical details of more than 500 000 people who lived in South Australia during the first fifty years of colonisation.

Biographical Register of the Victorian Parliament 1900–1984. Ed. Geoff Browne. Victorian Government Printing Office, Melbourne, 1985.

Dictionary of Australian Bushrangers. Ed. R. Mendham. Hawthorn Press, Melbourne, 1975.

Searle, P. *Dictionary of Australian Biography*, 2 vols. Angus and Robertson, Sydney, 1949.

Lists people from 1788 to 1942.

Who's Who in Australia, 1906–1988. Herald and Weekly Times, Melbourne, 1988. (Also microfiche to 1977.)
   Biographical information about notable Australians.

General primary and secondary works

The Australian Encyclopaedia, 12 vols. Grolier Society of Australia, Sydney, 1983.

Bateson, Charles. *The Convict Ships 1787–1868*. Brown, Son and Ferguson, Glasgow, 1969.
   An essential standard reference on ships that carried transportees from England and Ireland. Deals with their destinations: New South Wales 1787–1840, Port Phillip 1803 and 1844–1849, Van Diemen's Land (Tasmania) 1803–1853 and Western Australia 1850–1868. Gives names of surgeons and masters and departure and arrival dates.

Davidson, J., and Doxford, H. *Grave Reflections*, vol. 1: *An Alphabetical Listing of Burial Sites in the Central Goldfields Area of Victoria, with a Selection of Tombstones of Interest*. J. Davidson, and H. Doxford, Melbourne, 1983.

Historical Records of Australia, series I–IV, 33 vols. Ed. Frederick Watson. Library Committee of the Commonwealth Parliament, Sydney, 1914–1925.

Historical Records of New South Wales 1793–1901, 7 vols. Ed. F. M. Bladen. Lansdown Slattery, Mona Vale, 1979.

Historical Records of Victoria, 4 vols. Victorian Government Printing Office, Melbourne, 1981–1984.
   Excellent collection of records providing historical background on the beginnings of permanent settlement (vol. 1), the Aborigines of Port Phillip 1835–1839 and their Protectors (vols 2A and 2B), the early development of Melbourne 1836–1839 (vol. 3) and communications, trade and transport 1836–1839 (vol. 4).

Letters from Emigrants to Queensland 1863–1885. Queensland Family History Society, Indooroopilly, 1984.

Name Directory of Moreton Bay Region, 3 vols (1850–1851, 1852–1853, 1854–1855). Comp. Marianne Eastgate. Queensland Family History Society, Indooroopilly, 1984.

Open Day Papers: Queensland Research Guide, 1982; *Man on the Land*, 1985; *A Grave Look at Family History*, 1986; *Our Migratory Ancestors*, 1987. Queensland Family History Society, Indooroopilly, 1982–1987.

O'Sullivan, Jim F. *A Short Guide to Tracing Your Convict Ancestry*. Queensland Family History Society, Indooroopilly, 1985.

Strays Collection Australasia, 2 vols. Comp. Rae Hopkinson. Queensland Family History Society, Indooroopilly, 1985–1986.

Swain, Ann. *Directory of Family Names*. Queensland Family History Society, Indooroopilly, 1983, 1985 and 1987.

Writing and publishing family histories

Beaumont, Joanna. *How to Do Your Own Publishing*. Orlando Press, Sydney, 1984.
   A complete guide to self-publishing, dealing with such topics as how books

of personal computers and their components, including disk drives, printers and monitors. A useful glossary of computer terminology is included, as well as a most comprehensive listing of genealogical software packages available and the names and addresses of each supplier.

are published, the parts of a book, illustrations, typesetting, proofreading, making up the pages, the cover, printing and binding, promotion, advertising, selling, distribution, the book bounty and so on.

——. *How to Write and Publish Your Family History: A Complete Guide for Australia and New Zealand.* Orlando Press, Sydney, 1985.

A concise, practical guide on how to research and then write your family history, based on the 'time and topic approach', that is, on a combination of a straight chronological narrative and an account that takes up selected experiences and attitudes of a main character. The second half of the book is devoted to the promotion and production aspects of publishing your family history, including the more technical side. It gives clear diagrams of binding, type and so on and includes a glossary of technical terms and some useful addresses.

Daniel, Lois. *How to Write Your Own Life Story: A Step-by-step Guide for the Non-professional Writer.* Chicago Review Press, Chicago, 1980.

An excellent guide for the non-professional writer. It includes exercises to attempt before you commence writing the story of your life, as well as a list of other topics to write about.

Meadley, Dom. *Writing a Family History.* Australian Institute of Genealogical Studies, Oakleigh, 1985.

Provides excellent, clear and very readable guidelines to writing a family history and methods of pulling the manuscript together for publication. It includes sections on charts, writing the story, word processing, layout, preparation of the manuscript, publishing, indexing and important hints.

Reakes, Janet. *Leaves on the Family Tree: Ideas on How to Write the Family Story.* Genealogy Research Service Centre, Bass Hill, 1986.

Provides ideas on writing family history, including clear guidelines on interviewing relatives, organisation of notes, charts and so on.

Computers in genealogy

'Computers.' *Ancestor*, Autumn, 1987.

The article by the Victorian GUM provides an excellent, clear guide to buying a computer. It discusses three different categories of computer and the software options for each.

Hawgood, David. *Computers for Family History: An Introduction.* Hawgood Computing, London, 1985.

Written by a former editor of *Computers in Genealogy* magazine, it is geared to first-time computer users. It describes the computer equipment required, terminology used, types of information genealogists need to store and how computers can help. It also covers the three main areas of commercially available software packages useful to genealogists. A very informative, readable book.

Worthington, Janet R. *Computers for Genealogy: A Guide.* Janet R. Worthington, Sydney, 1985.

An excellent, clear guide on the whys, whens, hows and wheres of purchasing a computer. A checklist is provided to help you in your search for the right computer and software to meet your requirements. Covers the features

Journals, magazines and newspapers

Ancestor (formerly *Victorian Genealogist*). Quarterly journal of Genealogical Society of Victoria, Melbourne, 1955– .

Ancestral Searcher. Quarterly journal of Heraldry and Genealogy Society of Canberra, Canberra, 1976– .

Descent. Quarterly journal of Society of Australian Genealogists, Sydney, 1961– .

Genealogist. Quarterly journal of Australian Institute of Genealogical Studies, Melbourne, 1974– .

Generation. Quarterly journal of Genealogical Society of Queensland, Stones Corner, 1979– .

Progenitor. Quarterly journal of Genealogical Society of the Northern Territory, Darwin, 1982– .

Queensland Family Historian. Bi-monthly journal of the Queensland Family History Society, Indooroopilly.

South Australian Genealogist. Quarterly journal of South Australian Genealogy and Heraldry Society, Adelaide, 1974– .

Tasmanian Ancestry. Quarterly journal of Genealogical Society of Tasmania, Hobart, 1980– .

Western Ancestor. Quarterly journal of Genealogical Society of Western Australia, Perth, 1979– .

Newspapers in Australian Libraries. National Library of Australia, Canberra, 1985.
Lists all known files of newspapers available in Australia as at date of publication and indicates places where they are kept and the extent of the holdings.